AF598893

SKETCHBOOK TRAVELER

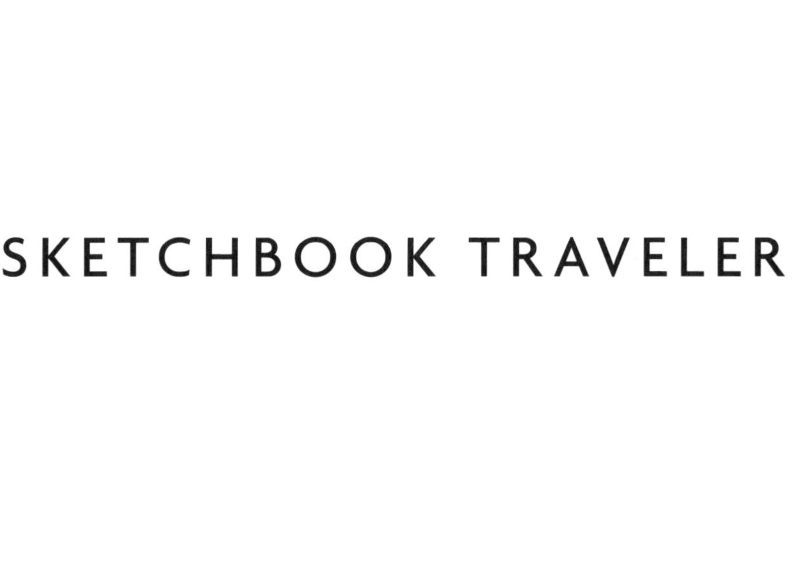

JAMES LANCEL MCELHINNEY

SKETCHBOOK TRAVELER

Hudson Valley

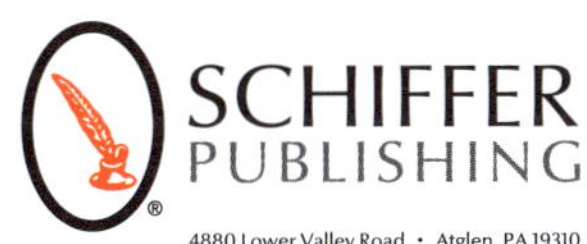

4880 Lower Valley Road • Atglen, PA 19310

Other Schiffer Books on Related Subjects:

The Art for Joy's Sake Journal: Watercolor Discovery and Releasing Your Creative Spirit, Kristy Rice, ISBN 978-0-7643-5767-1

Library of Congress Control Number: 2020930862

Designed by Ashley Millhouse
Type set in Agenda/Chronicle Text
ISBN: 978-0-7643-6042-8
Printed in China

Published by Schiffer Publishing, Ltd.
4880 Lower Valley Road
Atglen, PA 19310
Phone: (610) 593-1777; Fax: (610) 593-2002
E-mail: Info@schifferbooks.com
Web: www.schifferbooks.com

CONTENTS

Chapter 1

INTRODUCTION

Battling the elements during an ascent of Chimborazo in 1802, geographer and naturalist Alexander von Humboldt made mental notes of the flora clinging to its slopes—how similar they were to other plants living at comparable elevations. Battered by winds and snow, at more than 20,000 feet above sea level, the volcanic peak is farther from the Earth's core than anywhere else on the planet. While he never reached the mountaintop, Humboldt had a revelation. The unity of nature, as expressed by the relationship between living things and their environments, was an idea that would shape scientific practice for more than half a century.

Having met Humboldt in Paris, inspired by the scientist's ascent of Chimborazo, Simón Bolívar returned to South America, aflame with revolutionary fervor. In 1822, his forces were at war with Spain. One night as he slept, Bolívar experienced a vision of Gran Colombia. Ascending the mountain to behold it all, upon reaching the summit he meets Father Time. Mocking human vanity, the phantom sends him on his way, to tell the world what he has seen.

Take out a photo album. Turn on your computer. Find a photograph you took ten years ago. Perhaps you were on a mountaintop at the end of a long hike, touring ancient ruins, visiting a bustling city, walking along a remote beach, or in a historic village on market day. Try to remember. What time was it? Who was with you? What was the weather, temperature, barometric pressure, wind speed, elevation above sea level? What did you eat that morning, that evening? How did it feel? A passing breeze, the ground underfoot, scents borne on the wind; smoke from a distant hearth, aromas from a bakery, nearby kitchen, or wildflowers blooming near a path. What happened an hour before, or three hours after the photograph was taken? Try to remember. What motivated you to reach for your camera, to capture a moment that mostly now is forgotten? How much can you retrieve from that image? Show it to someone else. Ask them. What do they see in it? What do they feel? Alert to every detail, we can honor every moment with close attention, before its memory slips our grasp and is lost forever. As a companion to the reader's travel gear, this pocket guide will help to make the most of each and every experience met along the way.

> Travel is fatal to prejudice, bigotry, and narrow-mindedness . . .
> —Mark Twain, *The Innocents Abroad*, 1869

Life is often compared to a voyage. From "Gilgamesh" to Homer's "Odyssey," from the journeys of Ibn Jubayr or Marco Polo, to Jonathan Swift and Mark Twain, much of world literature describes people on the move. The earliest humans were peripatetic, following their game from one seasonal hunting ground to another. Some of these migratory hunter-gatherers settled on fertile, alluvial plains. Developing the art of cultivation, farmsteads grew into villages, then towns, cities, and civilizations. Trade began along the rivers, reaching later across the seas.

Traveling great distances, to holy sites like Bodh Gaya, Jerusalem, or Mecca, pilgrims pray for rich harvests, good health, or relief from disease. The faithful often travel in groups, for protection against bandits and other perils of the road. Lodging, food, and souvenirs sold along the way gave birth to the tourism and hospitality industry.

Explorers are a different breed of traveler. Embarking on dangerous missions, in search of raw materials, new lands, and untapped markets, historically these were military men or armed merchants traveling by sea, along overland trade routes, and into unknown regions.

Advances in marine engineering and navigational technology

expanded the reach of these adventurers. Answerable to governments or private investors, they kept detailed logs, produced maps and drawings, and at times, personal diaries.

During the eighteenth century a new form of vacation travel known as The Grand Tour was a boon to the hospitality industry in European cities, spas, and resorts. Travel books became bestsellers. Tourists filled their journals with writing and drawings, inspired by in expeditionary practice. The advent of steamships and railroads during the early nineteenth century expanded tourism to include a growing middle class. Artists like J. M. W. Turner, Carl Rottmann, J. B. C. Corot, and Eugene Delacroix were among the passengers traveling between northern Europe and Italy, Greece, and North Africa. Trekking with John Lloyd Stephens through the jungles of Central America, Frederick Catherwood gave us our first look at Mayan monuments. Frederic Edwin Church retraced Humboldt's travels into the heart of the equatorial Andes. Later he sailed to the Arctic, to paint icebergs from the rolling deck of a sailing ship. Church also traveled to Athens and Jerusalem, and into the Jordanian desert to Petra. Philip Gilbert Hamerton lived and painted in a portable hut, in the windswept Scottish Highlands. Traveling along Japan's North Sea Road, Andō Hiroshige produced a series of prints depicting the fifty-three stations of the Tōkaidō. Apart from artist-naturalists like Jacques le Moyne, Frans Post, Maria Sibylla Merian, John James Audubon, William Bartram, Margaret Mee, Marianne North, and Titian Ramsay Peale II, historic sketchbook travelers include such notables as Bruce Chatwin, Captain James Cook, Charles Darwin, Thor Heyerdahl, Sir Edmund Hillary, Louis Kahn, John Brinckerhoff Jackson, Auguste Morisot, and Ernest Shackleton. Most were on some kind of mission. Some were pilgrims. Some were explorers. At various times, most were both. Every morning, ask yourself: Which shall I be today, a pilgrim, or an explorer? Either answer will be correct.

Returning from his exploration of Latin American, Alexander von Humboldt stopped in the United States in 1804, to meet with the new republic's great men of science. Traveling with botanist Aimé Bonpland, he had produced his own maps and pictures. Visiting Monticello, Humboldt advised Thomas Jefferson to embed professional artists and scientists in future expeditions. The new military academy at West Point included two years of drawing in its curriculum, taught by professional painters. Military expeditions led by academy-trained topographical engineers included civilian draftsmen like Titian Ramsay Peale II and the brothers Kern, or soldier-artists like General Seth Eastman. Humboldt's advice was also taken to heart by a new generation of landscape painters, including Frederic Church, and later Albert Bierstadt and Thomas Moran, whose paintings of the West helped convince Congress to authorize new national parks. Automotive transportation a few decades later made traversing greater distances more affordable. Today with air travel, one can get from any point on the globe to another in less than twenty-four hours. Embarking on new journeys, ask yourself: Is the goal to reach a destination or follow a route just to see where it goes? Either way, personal mobility is a process. The more engaged in it we are, the richer our experience will be.

> I have always found that plans are worthless, but planning is indispensable.
> —Dwight D. Eisenhower (1890–1969)

Travel presents its own set of challenges, from simply getting from point A to point B, or being constantly in motion, with short breaks for meals and overnight stays. Many tourists just want to get from the airport to the hotel, grab a meal, and go shopping. This book is for people who want more. Below is a checklist to prep for mindful travel:

- Research your destination or itinerary. Learn about its people, flora, fauna, history, customs, art, music, literature, cuisine, and economy. What dangers might you face? What vaccines will you require? Dietary restrictions? Access to medical care?
- Acquire a basic knowledge of the language. Learn a few key phrases. Plan to learn more once boots are on the ground.
- Study maps of the region or route. What kind of terrain will you be crossing? By what means will you travel? What towns or cities will be on your itinerary? Traversing different regions, focus on specific settings. How do they differ from one another?
- Having considered all of the above, what kind of places beckon you? Which places do you need to visit? Approach every day as a bucket list event. Make a plan, but stay nimble. Be ready to improvise.

> By failing to prepare, you are preparing to fail.
> —Benjamin Franklin (1706–1790)

A cardinal rule for carrying supplies in and out of natural settings is *Leave No Trace*. Only bring what you need. Leave nothing behind. Whatever you forgot to bring, or need to replace can be purchased along the way. Apart from clothing, footwear, and toiletries, most people travel with a camera, or at least a mobile phone with a photo app. You might upload an audio recorder app onto your phone or tablet, or bring a separate voice recorder for dictation. Carrying electronics means they have to be powered up on a daily basis, sometimes more frequently. Pack one or two portable power packs, with device-appropriate cords or cables. Your gear should also include a pocket notebook (such as the book now in your hand), and some form of writing implements. All of this will be covered in detail in the pages to follow.

> I never travel without my diary. One should always have something sensational to read on the train.
>
> —Oscar Wilde (1854–1900)

The importance of keeping a journal cannot be understated. Writing by hand has the effect of inscribing durable memories onto the human hard drive, far beyond data-retrieval technologies that merely simulate experience. Photography is an art form, but few people practice it with such finesse and ambition. The same is true of drawing and writing. Drawing is just a form of writing that employs a visual language. One need not be a poet or playwright to scribble a shopping list, nor a brilliant draftsman to chart visual sensations. Either way, whatever lands on the page is far less important than engaging in a cognitive-sensory activity that transforms experience into knowledge. Embracing an expeditionary spirit, quotidian journals receive daily entries, beginning with the date, day of the week, and year, followed by location name, map coordinates, and weather. A trick used by some historical travel writers was to make a list of notable events as they happened, and then fill in the details later. Appearing as chapter headings in published narratives, such lists gave readers something like a movie trailer of what is to follow. One may prefer to flesh out their impressions in real time or at their leisure sometime in the future. The goal is to preserve, with great clarity, the most ephemeral sensations.

> Anyone that can learn to write can learn to draw.
>
> —John Gadsby Chapman, *American Drawing Book*, 1847

Few travelers are shy about keeping a diary, but many are hesitant to draw, believing it to be the genius domain of talented artists. In fact, drawing is no different than playing a musical instrument. One may do it for pleasure, without having to be a concert-hall virtuoso, rockstar, or jazz legend. Journal drawing requires attention, but is no more difficult than pitching a tent, lighting a campfire, or packing a parachute. The best way to translate visual experience into marks on paper is to think of it as a kind of mapping. The task is to teach yourself what you behold by picturing where you are.

> What is it about maps? I could look at them all day, earnestly studying the names of towns and villages I have never heard of and will never visit.
>
> —Bill Bryson (b. 1951)

Orienteering is the art of pathfinding across unfamiliar terrain. The process of orienting a map aligns the chart with compass-readings to locate your position. West = Occident, North = Boreas, South = Antipodean. It can also mean to face east. In map-reading, to orient is to find your position on a map. Making observations requires that first you know where you are. Traveling in well-marked areas and carrying a map, the task is simple. If not, you may have to determine your location by triangulation; from your position, take compass readings for sight vectors to prominent landmarks, and then plot your position on the map. But what if you don't have a map?

Having no charts of the Missouri River, when Lewis and Clark set off in a keelboat in 1804, the Corps of Discovery was forced to rely on a few unverified maps, and a semiliterate assortment of trappers and river guides. Assisted by his African American manservant York, second-in-command William Clark managed to conduct a detailed survey of their route, using basic instruments.

Clark's zigzag lines are flanked by two sets of numbers: map headings and distances. Reading a compass, Clark would measure a directional sight vector between his position and a target, while York paced off the distance. Sometimes York himself was the landmark. The map Clark later produced became the most accurate picture of the Northern Plains and Pacific Northwest of its time. Prints of it were carried by expeditioners, traders, and travelers, whose reports Clark would use to update and add detail to his original map. Clark freed York after the expedition, and set him up with a freight-hauling business. Legend claims that York returned upriver, where he lived out his days among other people of color.

> Drawing is all curved lines and straight lines. Anyone can draw a curved line. Anyone can draw a straight line. Therefore, anyone can draw.
> —Thomas Gimbrede (1781–1832), drawing master, USMA-West Point

The only difference between maps and pictures is point of view. Cartography envisions the Earth as it might be seen from the heavens. In the days before air and space travel, these visions could only be imagined. Pictures are nothing more than maps of what is visible from the ground. If you can find your location on a map, you should be able to draw what is before you. Take your time. Drawing is a slow art, a form of meditation, a way to graduate from looking to seeing. Always begin with quick, broad strokes. First, find your horizon on the page. Quickly note the locations of three focal points. Measure the distance between them. Drawings are just collections of straight lines and curved lines—movements and measurements filling the page. Hold the pencil loosely, far from the point when you begin. As the drawing comes into focus, take a firmer grip to direct the line with greater precision. Good drawings balance energy and clarity. Try not to be fussy. Pay attention. It's not about making art but creating a durable memory.

> Painting is poetry that is seen rather than felt.
> Poetry is painting that is felt rather than seen.
> —Leonardo da Vinci (1452–1519)

Visiting Italy a few years ago, Kathie and I were invited to a jazz-sitar concert at Palazzo Dona Dalle Rosa. Standing inconspicuously to the side, I took out a pen and a sketchbook. I began to draw the whole room, then later focused on the musicians. After pausing to drain a glass of Prosecco, I began to make candid portraits of other audience members. A British gentleman came up behind me, looking over my shoulder. He was visiting Venice on a fellowship, doing research on the history of private gardens of Stella Maris. Confessing to me that he almost never drew, he proudly added that he carried a pocket notebook in which he would form with words impressions of his surroundings. Finding a quiet place, free of distractions and interruptions, absorbing the ambience and character of his location, he would compose an evocation of the moment. Better than a diary, I noted. "Yes," he replied. "It's my version of your sketchbook."

> To lose a passport was the least of one's worries.
> To lose a notebook was a catastrophe.
> —Bruce Chatwin (1940–1989)

Travel is not just the act of crossing the earth. Every journey transforms us. Having the gift of mobility allows us to change our surroundings. Passing from one destination to another, we experience more than just the pleasing effect of scenery or disagreeable visions of dystopic blight. Moving in footsteps, or at high speeds, we traverse not only land, but cultures, communities, peoples, wildlife, and flora; climate zones, geological formations, political, and economic systems. Slow down. Take notice of it all.

- Be your own travel writer. Greet every day as a new episode in your unfolding story. Make lists, gather facts, and take notes. Be succinct. Keep a daily log. Sketch out your day's events, movements, meals, and sights. At the end of the day, make time to unpack it all into a narrative. Before long you will begin to develop a voice.

- Be a cartographer. Draw your own maps. One of the joys of global positioning technology is that any one of a number of apps can provide us with map coordinates in a simple pin drop. Note where and when you were at different locations throughout the course of the day. Weave these details into your story.
- Be an expeditionary draftsman. Writing down your impressions, also make drawings. Ignore any feeling of pressure to make art. Imagine that what you behold is seen through a viewfinder. Where is your horizon? Mark the locations of major features. Think of the page as a tablet, letting you inscribe the experience onto your memory.
- Having a plan will prepare you to improvise. Apart from creating an itinerary, be sure to carry a list of local contacts, your national consulate or embassy, local emergency medical services, healthcare facilities, and law enforcement agencies. Identify any medical conditions you may have in case you are unable to advocate for yourself in the event of an emergency. There are also protocols for the evacuation of mortal remains should the trip prove to be your last. Having thought of everything, you can put your mind at rest and start enjoying your next adventure.

> When you are everywhere, you are nowhere.
> When you are somewhere, you are everywhere.
> —Jalal al-Din Muhammad Rumi (1207–1273)

Where we are is not a fact, but a state of mind. The more conscious we are of our surroundings, the more productive will be our rapport with the environment. Mindfulness not only enriches our experience of nature; in some instances, it is a prerequisite for success. How often do fishermen see trout leap from the stream, into a frying pan? How many prospectors were discovered by golden nuggets?

Being mindful can save our lives. Hiking at Joshua Tree National Park, I met a large rattlesnake crossing the trail. We parted without incident. Walking back to the parking area, I passed a college-aged group heading up the trail. Mostly dressed for the beach, one or two wore flip-flops. Warned about the snake, they seemed less concerned about the danger than seeing a deadly serpent. Coming down off the plateau into Twenty-Nine Palms, I stopped at the visitor center.

A park ranger explained, "We have seven kinds of rattlers here. The one you just saw delivers a triple-threat cocktail of hemotoxin, neurotoxin, and muscle relaxant. They're very efficient hunters, but won't mess with you unless you bother them first." Believe it or not, few visitors get bitten. On the other hand, folks who run their dogs off the leash are liable to lose a pet. Environmental awareness has become a top priority, not only for nature lovers, but for anyone concerned about the preservation of natural resources. Venturing out into nature or visiting unfamiliar places, can expose travelers to certain risks. Be well informed about your destinations, taking all necessary precautions, in order to be prepared to face any challenge you might meet.

The next step toward becoming more fully engaged with your surroundings is to break out of your comfort zone. Take flight from the familiar.

The mindful traveler must be fearless enough to take the time to slow down, look around, open a sketchbook, and start drawing. Even the most practiced draughtsman can find this experience humbling. There could be no better evidence of this than the words of the great Japanese artist Katsuchika Hokusai, writing at age seventy-five.

> "From the age of six, I had a mania for drawing the shapes of things. At the age of fifty I had published an infinity of designs. But all I have done before the age of seventy is not worth taking into account. At seventy-three I learned a little about the real structure of nature, of animals, plants, trees, birds, fish, and insects. In consequence when I am eighty, I shall have made still more progress; at ninety I shall penetrate the mystery of things, at a hundred, I shall certainly have reached a marvelous stage; and when I am a hundred and ten, everything I do, whether it be a dot or a line, will be alive. I beg those who live as long as I to see if I do not keep my word. Signed, 'Old Man Mad about Drawing.'"

A passion for learning, a curious mind, and a patient eye will always be rewarded, even more when one inspires oneself to devotion. John Burroughs (1837–1921) was a key figure in the American environmentalist movement. While John Muir championed the spectacular western landscape, Burroughs celebrated the wondrous beauty and precious truths revealed by nature through close observation. In his essay "The Art of seeing Things" he writes,

> To know is not all; it is only half.
> To love is the other half.

Chapter 2

THE HUDSON VALLEY

On August 17, 1809, a curious craft was seen moving upriver. In place of sails, bystanders saw only a tall iron stack, belching black smoke, as a pair of waterwheels churned through the waves. Within a few years, hundreds of steamboats plied the Hudson River between New York and Albany. Within a few decades, rail service revolutionized public transit in the Empire State. Among the first travelers to avail themselves of these advancements were poets, artists, and writers, like Washington Irving, Louisa Davis Minot, Joshua Rowley Watson, William Guy Wall, Samuel F. B. Morse, James Fenimore Cooper, Thomas Cole, Asher B. Durand, William Cullen Bryant, Eliza Pratt Greatorex, Nathaniel Parker Willis, Frederic Edwin Church, Albert Bierstadt, Benson J. Lossing, and a legion of others.

The Hudson Valley provided soaring highlands and sweeping vistas that embodied nascent visions of Manifest Destiny then shaping the new republic. The Hudson River school is called the first American art movement. An insatiable appetite for spectacular scenes of wild places motivated ordinary citizens to witness for themselves the wonders and terrors of nature. Despite its dangers, suddenly the great outdoors became nature's classroom. The observation of geology, flora, and fauna improved the mind, while hiking, swimming, and canoeing strengthened the body. Great camps were built in the Adirondacks. While some preferred to sleep under the stars, others set up camp in sprawling hotels, perched on mountain ledges. After a day of roughing it in the field, guests could sit down to supper, clad in formal dinner attire. Times have changed.

With the formation of the Palisades Interstate Park in 1900, at the dawn of automotive transportation, and with the completion of the Appalachian Trail in 1937, the Hudson Valley, and especially its wild spaces, have become more accessible. The designation of the Hudson River Valley National Heritage Area in 1996, and the completion of the Empire State Trail in 2020 provide citizens and visitors with greater access to outdoor recreation. Private foundations such as the Hudson River Valley Greenway, Scenic Hudson, and the Sloop Clearwater complement these public resources through advocacy, interpretation, and program funding. Historic sites and artist's homes such as Ever Rest (Jasper F. Cropsey), Sunnyside (Washington Irving), Locust Grove (Samuel Morse), Thomas Cole House, and Olana (Frederic Edwin Church) all bear witness to the Hudson Valley's power to inspire enduring works of beauty and genius.

At a rate of flow averaging 3 miles per hour, a specific volume of water takes one week to move from the source of the river to the sea. Intermittently navigable above the tidewater stretch of the river, the Hudson is fraught with treacherous tides and currents. Its indigenous name Mahicannituck is translated as "waters that are never still," or "the river that flows both ways." Its 507-mile journey begins in a wilderness known to the Haudenosaunee people as Ra-tir-ron-tack or Bark-Eaters, in contempt for enemy tribes who inhabited the region.

Tumbling down from Lake Tear of the Clouds and the slopes of Mount Marcy, a confluence of mountain streams meet the west fork of the Hudson at Newcomb, the burial place of legendary Adirondack guide Mitchell Sabbatis. In 1859 travel writer and draughtsman Benson Lossing and his young bride were led by Sabbatis, to the highest summit in the Adirondacks. Mrs. Lossing was said to be only the second nonindigenous woman to ascend the mountain. By the time Lossing published *The Hudson from the Mountains to the Sea* in 1866, wild spaces across America were being invaded by trappers, loggers, and miners; sportsmen; and plein air painters. At the same time the Lossing party was climbing Mount Marcy, Winslow Homer painted a sketching group, lined up like fence posts, on a windswept hillside in the White Mountains. Homer also was fond of the Adirondacks. Sabbatis was often his guide.

From Newcomb whitewater rafting tours today descend the river, which flows south, and then east, rushing through deep ravines and steep valleys. The river again turns south. Farther on it is joined by the Sacandaga, near the villages of Hadley and Luzerne. Proceeding on to Glens Falls—the first and largest in a series of cataracts descending to the head of navigation 40 miles downstream—the Hudson bisects a wide alluvial plain, fed by tributaries with names like Battenkill and Hoosic. Shadowed and crisscrossed by the Champlain Canal, the river flows close to settlements made famous by James Fenimore Cooper's Leatherstocking Tales. Under foot of Stark's Knob, passing the bluffs of Bemis Heights, the river drifts past the open field where a British army surrendered, a boost to the Patriot cause, and a turning point in the Revolution. Downriver at the lower falls, the Hudson becomes a tidal estuary into which pours the Mohawk River, over the Falls of Cohoes, which once rivaled Niagara as a tourist attraction.

Below the Capital District of Albany, Rensselaer, and Troy, the river is fed by tributaries named Kaaterskill and Stockport, Rondout, Esopus, and Wappinger.

From the hilltop of Olana, the Hudson stretches southward as a serpentine ribbon of light. The eastern face of the Catskill escarpment stands off to the west, with Shawangunk Ridge beyond. Breaking the southern horizon, The Highlands rise a thousand feet, where Fishkill and Moodna Creeks drain into Newburgh Bay. Along the way, the river passes open spaces like Tivoli Bays and Poets' Walk.

Offering breathtaking views, an 1889 steel-truss railroad bridge crossing a narrow stretch of the river at Poughkeepsie reopened for pedestrian traffic in 2009. The cities of Newburgh and Beacon face one another across Newburgh Bay. Both are undergoing a renaissance.

Artists and entrepreneurs have revitalized local economies, developing waterfront attractions and recreational open spaces. Sloop Clearwater's home port is Beacon, whose most famous resident, the late folk singer Pete Seeger, was a powerful voice in promoting environmental priorities.

Beyond Dennngs Point, below Plum Point and Cornwall, the river enters a bottleneck.

Carving a path through the Ramapo section of the Appalachian range, over countless millennia, the river shaped one of the few true fjords in North America. Past Storm King, Breakneck Mountain, Crow's Nest, and the village of Cold Spring, the Hudson turns sharply eastward, around Constitution Island, and then south again, around Trophy Point. Above the right bank is US Military Academy at West Point. To the east, on a bluff above Constitution Marsh Audobon Center and Sanctuary stands Boscobel House and Garden, boasting one of the most picturesque views of the river. Looking south, one finds Anthony's Nose, Thunder Hill, and Bear Mountain and its namesake bridge, where the Appalachian Trail crosses the Hudson.

Flowing out of the Highlands South Gate past Roa Hook, the river flows through Peekskill Bay, around Stony Point into Haverstraw Bay. The Tors and Hook Mountains rise up from the western shore. Preserved as part of the Palisades Interstate Park system, the vertiginous highlands are traversed by hiking trails. To the east, a large finger of land extends across the river, separating Haverstraw Bay from Tappan Zee. Croton Point is now a county park. Just south of it on the eastern shore, Croton River flows west from Taconic Ridge, spilling into Tappan Zee. Sleepy Hollow and Tarrytown on the left bank face Nyack on the western shore. A few miles downstream, Piermont jetty juts into the river, next to a marsh at the mouth of Sparkill Creek.

A mile farther south, Tallman Bluff is maintained as a park, anchoring the northern end of a wall of basalt columns, stretching south to Weehawken, New Jersey. A strip of deciduous woodland has found purchase amid giant heaps of rockfall at the foot of the palisades. Atop the palisades, the historic Long Path has led travelers between Fort Lee, New Jersey, and the mountains of Ulster County, New York. Large portions remain in use. Across the river, stately homes of patriots, poets, and robber-barons stand on the eastern shore. Passing Dobbs Ferry, Hastings-on-Hudson, Yonkers, and Riverdale, the river continues past Spuyten Duyvill Creek. Located on a major avian migratory flyway, the hills of northern Manhattan attract large numbers of birdwatchers. They also hold one of the last stands of native forest in the region. Champion trees can be found up and down the valley. Some of them can be found at Inwood Hill.

As natural terrain disappears beneath the Anthropocene facsimile of a coral reef, the river makes its way into the harbor, past Manhattan, Hoboken, and Paulus Hook. The Hackensack River flows in from the northwest, between Bayonne and Staten Island. Past Brooklyn, through The Narrows, past Gateway beaches and Coney Island, the Hudson melts into Raritan Bay. Beyond Sandy Hook, the great North River finally disappears into the Atlantic Ocean.

As the mountain brook becomes a stream, the creek becomes a river. Racing through canyons, over falls and rapids, flowing through alpine glades, valleys, bays, and harbors, each mile of its journey is rich with history, legend, and lore. The river that never stands still awaits. Pack your bags. The Hudson is calling.

Chapter 3
LESSONS IN PRINT

Among the advantages of sketchbook journaling is that fewer people will notice that you are drawing or painting. Someone working at an easel is an instant magnet for curiosity seekers. Some of the questions people ask can be hilarious:

- You really do that for a living?
- How much will you get for that?
- Who are you doing that for?
- How long have you been working on that?
- What are you doing?
- (and my personal favorite)
- You do mean shade, dude. You could do tattoo.

One can sense them trying to reckon an hourly rate from your answers. Studying at the Skowhegan School of Painting and Sculpture in Maine one summer, I accompanied a plein air group led by New York painter Paul Resika to one of the nearby mill towns. Painting by the dam, an elderly couple approached him. Dressed all in white, with a white hat, white espadrilles, and a bushy black beard, Paul was straight from central casting for a biopic of Claude Monet. The couple asked him if they could take a peek at his work. Removing his hat with a flourish, he extended it to them, like a mendicant's bowl. Thus rebuffed, they hurried away. Drawing or painting in public places may attract unwanted attention. Accept it. That comes with the territory. My response to curiosity-seekers is to be polite but diffident at first. I may show someone a page spread, but I never let them handle the book or my tools. I might ask them if they are interested in travel, drawing, or painting. If they want to ask me about my process, I'm happy to engage them in conversation. On rare occasions, I might exchange business cards with them, to continue the conversation later. Being open to meeting new people is a prerequisite of mindful travel. Much can be learned from the locals, as well as from fellow pilgrims and explorers.

Wherever you go, behave like a guest. Be patient and courteous. In certain settings, like Indian reservations, drawing and photography is forbidden without permission. Permits are generally available at the tribal governor's office for a fee. Some religious sites forbid photography or making pictures of any kind. Be sure to ask.

I sat one day in Cologne cathedral, drawing the polychrome wooden statue of Saint Christopher that clings to one of its column. Suddenly the tranquility was pierced by the ringtone of a mobile phone. A smartly dressed woman answered it, "Hallo?" Silently from out of the shadows, tall men draped in long red robes materialized beside her and lifted her up by the elbows to sweep her down the aisle and out the door.

In some parts of the world, people come into the city from the countryside, dressed in traditional ethnic garb. If you want to draw them, be prepared to pay them. In certain countries, it might be very unwise to be seen making drawings near or around military and government installations, dams, power stations, tunnels, and bridges. Do your research. Know where you are. Obey local laws and customs. Maintain a modest profile. To have a positive productive experience with your surroundings, avoid conflict with them.

FIND A MOTIF

> The clouds will not wait while we copy their heaps or clefts; the shadows will escape from us as we try to shape them, each, in its stealthy minute march, still leaving light where its tremulous edge had rested the moment before, and involving in eclipse objects that had seemed safe from its influence; and instead of the small clusters of leaves which we could reckon point by point, embarrassing enough even though numerable, we have now leaves as little to be counted as the sands of the sea, and restless, perhaps, as its foam.
> —John Ruskin (1819–1900)

The best places to pause, take notes, or to draw should always take you by surprise. Too many people march past what might be personal favorites on their way to bucket-list vistas. Landscape painters refer to their subjects as motifs—opportune arrangements of topography, weather, and foliage that suggest a composition. Searching for motifs is like prospecting for gold. A telltale twinkle in a pan full of wet silt tells us to unpack our mules and get to work.

I have spent many afternoons working in my journal, only to turn my head in a new direction to behold an even better subject. The landscape is not what's out there, but what's inside you.

> Landscapes do not occur in nature,
> but are created when humans adapt terrain to their use.
> —John Brinckerhoff Jackson (1909–1996)

In planning a trip, identify your destination and estimate the duration of your visit and travel time required. Acquaint yourself with maps, travel guides for your destination, field guides to wildlife, plants, and geology. Know the history of your destination and its region. Create an equipment checklist. Make sure to pack everything you will need. Check the weather prior to departure. Make appropriate adjustments of supplies, clothing, and equipment. Identify an emergency contact. Let them know your travel plans. Carry their contact information on your person. Travel with a companion, or just go it alone. Once on site, follow your plan, but be prepared to improvise. Get off the beaten path, but keep track of your location. Keep an eye on the time. Set aside one to three hours at each stop to take in your surroundings, to write and draw. Take your time. Savor the journey. Carry in, carry out. Leave everything you encounter just as you found it.

WRITE WHAT YOU SEE

Turning sensations into marks on the page, as words, pictures, or both, imprints durable memories onto the human hard-drive, transforming experience into knowledge and ideas.

Do not be intimidated by the challenge of drawing or believe for a moment that you lack the talent to succeed. Whatever you commit to the page is for your benefit.

If your drawings do not attain the level of art, the process will connect you more profoundly with what you behold. Your words may not ascend the lofty heights of literature, but if they bring you in closer dialogue with your surroundings they will be just as worthy.

A visual journal contains two kinds of drawings: pictures and writing. Each requires the same degree of attention, focus, and patience. Technically, they differ greatly. Holding a pencil to write is not the best way to hold a pencil to draw. Handwriting requires a measured regularity of movement and pressure, whereas finding an image begins with a question.

> Writing is nothing else than drawing the forms of letters.
> Drawing is little more but writing the forms of objects.
> —Rembrandt Peale (1778–1860)

Lesson One

Holding the Pencil. Place the butt end of the pencil in the palm of your hand, lay your index finger upon its side, pointing toward the tip. Rest the pencil between your thumb and bent middle finger. Alternately, you might rest both your first and second finger on the pencil, with its shaft between them.

Lesson Two

Line Pressure and Darkness. To begin, hold the pencil with its point as far from your hand as possible. Grasp the butt end of the pencil between your thumb, index, and middle fingers. Sketch lightly, loosely, with mostly indefinite marks. Instead of drawing a solid line, you might make a chain of dots or dashes, to be connected later. As your drawing develops and you become more certain of what to put down, move your grip closer to the point, which will darken your line.

Lesson Three

Define the Frame. First look at your subject. Make a decision to work within either a portrait or landscape format. To begin, first draw the frame of a rectangle. Put the point of your pencil on the page, at the desired distance from the edge. With the hand holding the pencil, place the edge(s) of the book in the notch inbetween your second and third fingertips, letting your hand glide from one edge of the page to the other. The shape of the sketchbook should never dictate the shape of your work. Quickly define the proportions of the rectangle, or whatever shape you wish the frame to be.

Lesson Four

Straight Lines. As a warmup exercise before drawing, draw any number of straight lines in as many different directions as possible. In drawing, a line can represent several ideas; a division, a trajectory, or a connection. Using a ruler to draw straight lines bypasses the brain. Learn how to use your body as a mechanical device. Put two dots on the page, some distance apart. Then try to connect them with a straight line. Do not look at the pencil. Look at the dots. Put the tip of the pencil on one dot. Looking at the other dot, use the tip of the pencil to bring them together. This is the same principle as shooting a rifle. If your grip, body, and breathing are in perfect alignment, the bullet will hit its mark. Practice makes perfect.

Lesson Five

Curved Lines. Another warmup exercise is to fill a page with curved lines. The first few times you try this, you will notice that all of the curves are identical. The reason for this is that our hand and wrist are in fact a kind of compass. Changing the grip from a writing position to a pointing or drawing positon will yield similar results. Study that open curve. It is your enemy. If you find that kind of curved line in a drawing, it means you were not really looking, but allowing your body to decide what mark to make. Practice drawing different kinds of curves. How many can you invent? Approach these processes like play, not like training for gold at the Olympics.

Lesson Six

Laws of Quadrants and Thirds. If drawing is all curved lines and straight lines, then pictorial composition—designing the picture—is all about movements and measurement, motion and rest. If this sounds like music, it is. Motion and rest are represented by two basic concepts: dynamism and balance, expressed as symmetry and asymmetry. Some refer to this as the "anatomy of the rectangle." Having decided which format, (portrait or landscape) and what shape (square, rectangular, or panoramic), you need to take a look at the muscle, guts, and bones inside the frame.

A. Law of Quadrants. Divide your rectangle four ways. Draw straight lines connecting opposite corners. Where they cross is dead center on the page. Drop a vertical through this point. Through it, then draw a horizontal, clear across the page. You will see four new rectangles, each identical in proportion to the shape they just divided. This represents symmetry. Make sure that whatever each of these contains has a different character from all the rest. While you want stability, you also want a lively image.

B. Law of Thirds. Draw a line between one end of the center horizontal line dividing the top quadrants from the bottom two, and the upper corner opposite. Where this line crosses the diagonal drawn to

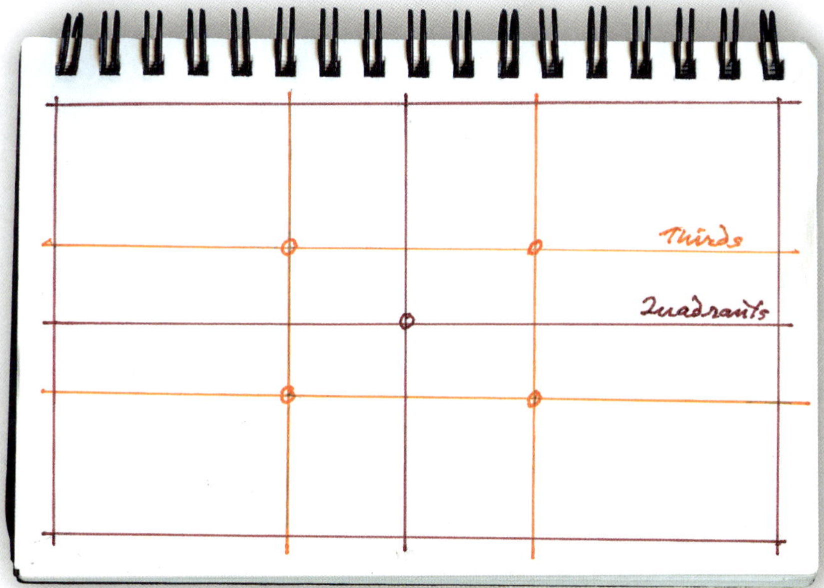

find the center, make a dot. Drop a vertical through in to the diagonal below. Next draw horizontals from this point past the center of the page to the other diagonals. Make dots as before. Those who are familiar with old SLR cameras will recognize these four dots from the viewfinders of old cameras. These points are used to target subjects, as a way to avoid centering an image in a static composition.

Lesson Seven

Finding the Image. First locate the horizon. This represents your point of view—the boundary between what is up and what is down, as seen from your perspective. Next, identify four or five major features or landmarks. Do not render their shapes. Just mark their locations. Verify the layout of your drawing by projecting straight lines between these points, like vectors in mapping. Again, sketching lightly, try to discover movements in the topography, like the terrain rising to a hilltop, or the course of a river or stream. Your goal is to draw the space, not individual rocks, trees, or clouds. Go back and use vectors again, to check your measurements. You can follow this method down to the smallest detail. Always begin your drawing with the largest forms, never with the details. Drawing is not a technique. It is writing down what you behold. When first we look at a landscape, we take in a sweeping vista, then slowly discover smaller features. It's only natural to unpack a drawing in precisely the same way.

Lesson Eight

Light and Shadow. Once you are competent with this process and gain some confidence in rapid sketching, you might take notes with a pen or brush, in black and white. Using a pencil lets you correct, but in experiential drawing there are no mistakes, only decisions. If you prefer the feeling of drawing with a pencil, do not use an eraser. Write down what you behold in real time, as you take notice of one thing, and then another. Think of the page like a tablet, a mode of transmission. The only drawings that matter are those inscribed onto your memory bank. They teach you what you behold. When you know something, you will be able to draw it. It's about the process, not the product. A drawing is an experience made visible.

Lesson Nine

Working en Grisaille. Value, or tone, includes black and white, at opposite ends of a gray scale. Working en plein air, think of your palette like a kind of keyboard that includes five shades of gray, plus black. Think of black and white as colors. Monochrome is a color scheme, one that has played an illustrious role in Asian art for more than a thousand years. In French, the word for a black-and-white painting is *grisaille.* With transparent media like ink and watercolor, always work from the lightest value to the darkest. Leave blank any area of the page that is to remain white. Begin with a larger brush, finish with a smaller brush.

Lesson Ten

Color. British portrait painter Sir Joshua Reynolds is said to have started working in a darkened room, his sitter barely visible. As the work developed, the painter would draw back the curtains an inch at a time, until light filled the room. Using value or color can add greatly to your drawing experience. It also presents certain challenges. Our first response is to match colors, then color in the drawing. This takes us on a detour from the experience at hand. Visual recognition instincts are essential survival skills. In drawing they become roadblocks to learning what we behold. Drawing lets us tackle the space. Painting does the same for light.

> In nature light makes color, in painting, color makes light.
> —Hans Hoffmann (1530–1591)

Adding color to a drawing is like bringing another musical instrument into an ensemble. Painting is a *pas de deux*, the marriage of drawing and color. The goal in painting is not to color the drawing, but to draw with color. For fieldwork, two basic color concepts are essential.

Lesson Eleven

Warm and Cool Color. Color temperature is the contrast between cool and warm colors. Warm colors include yellow, orange, and red. Cool colors include any shade of blue and some grays, when contrasted with warm colors. Green and violet can go both ways. For fieldwork, it is best to select a pair of opposing complements, like blue/orange or violet/yellow because these also represent shifts in value; blue = dark, orange = light, likewise purple = dark, and yellow = light. On the color wheel, red and green are too close in value.

Lesson Twelve

Look, See, Remember. If you have already selected a monochromatic palette, follow through. Stay with it. Do not change direction by introducing a warm-cool color scheme. If you have decided on a chromatic work, begin by selecting a pair of contrasting colors and laying them down in broad, light washes. Never try to finish a painting in the field. Take notes. Unzip the file back at camp, in your hotel room, or at home. Working in the field, we look at the subject and try to memorize its forms and colors. Then we look back at the page and try to draw what we just beheld. Even when we are working in front of our subject, we are always drawing from memory. Consult your own photographs. Do not copy them. Use them only as reminders.

> We made several photos which will give me all the details I want if I conclude to paint the view.
> —Thomas Moran (1837–1926)

Great film directors like Sergei Eisenstein and Akira Kurosawa drew their own storyboards. Keeping a visual journal and handwritten log is a way to storyboard your adventures.

Landscape and nature photographers will find that journal-drawing and painting en plein air will expand and enrich their own practice. Expeditionary photographer William Henry Jackson began his career as a painter. Renowned photojournalist Henri Cartier-Bresson was an accomplished draughtsman. Today everyone carries a camera to capture memories. Carrying a sketchbook in a pocket, backpack, or briefcase will not only improve your photography by developing new skills, it will also build your visual muscle. Make it part of your daily routine. It will enhance the pleasures of travel, by focusing your encounters with faraway destinations, and the wonders of nature. Finding yourself in an elegant bistro, or on the rim of a wild canyon, a sketchbook becomes your home away from home—an office in your pocket. Like your mobile phone, but with one notable exception: The only power source it needs is *you*.

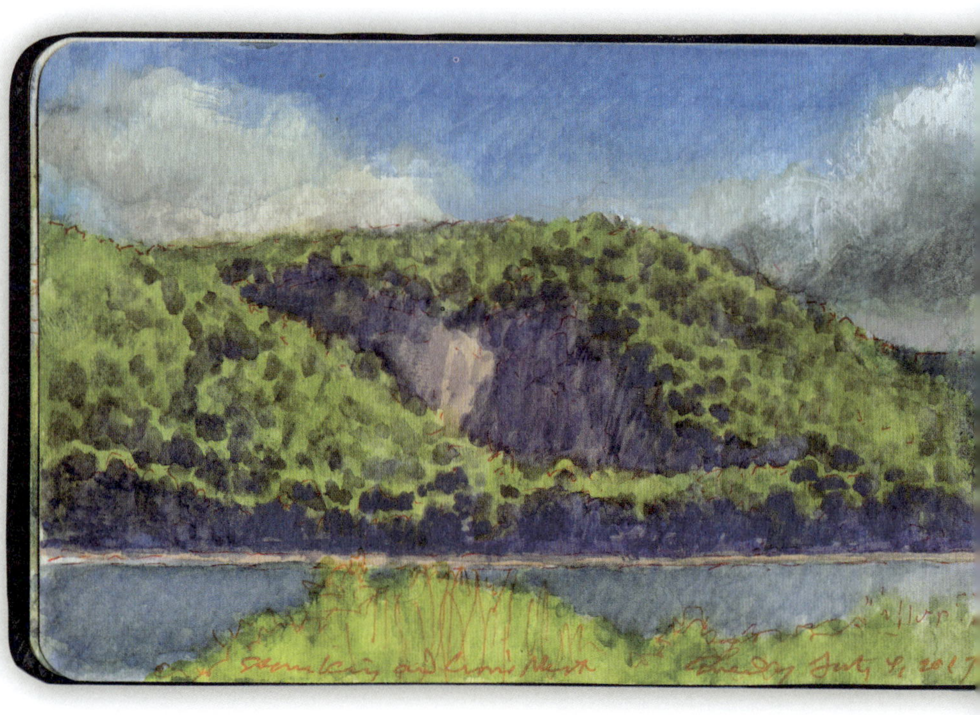

Chapter 4

GALLERY IN PRINT: JOURNAL PAGES

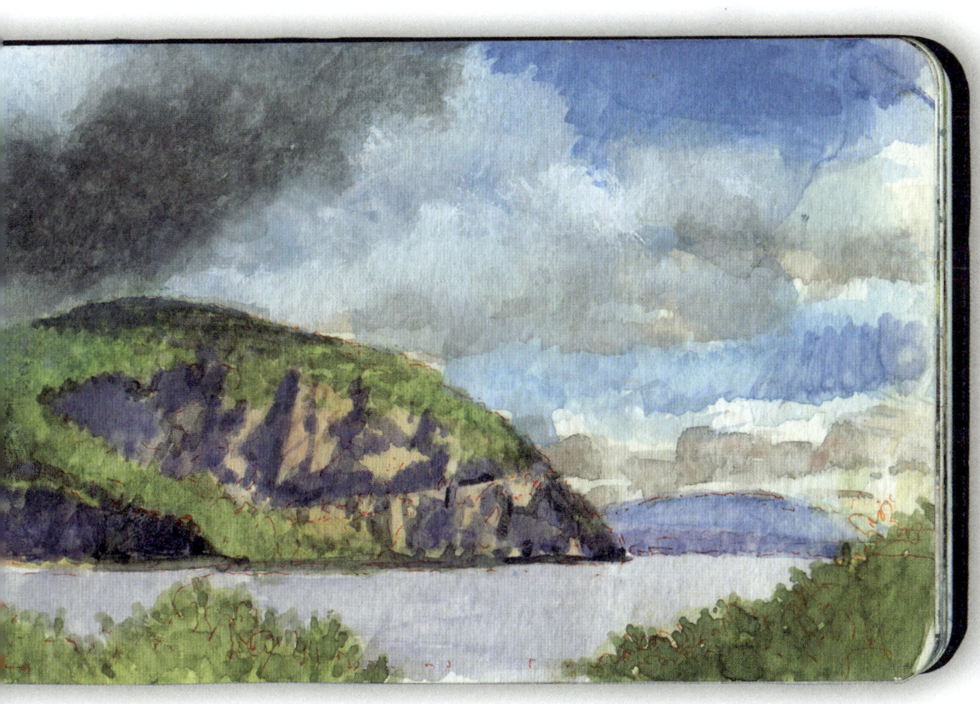

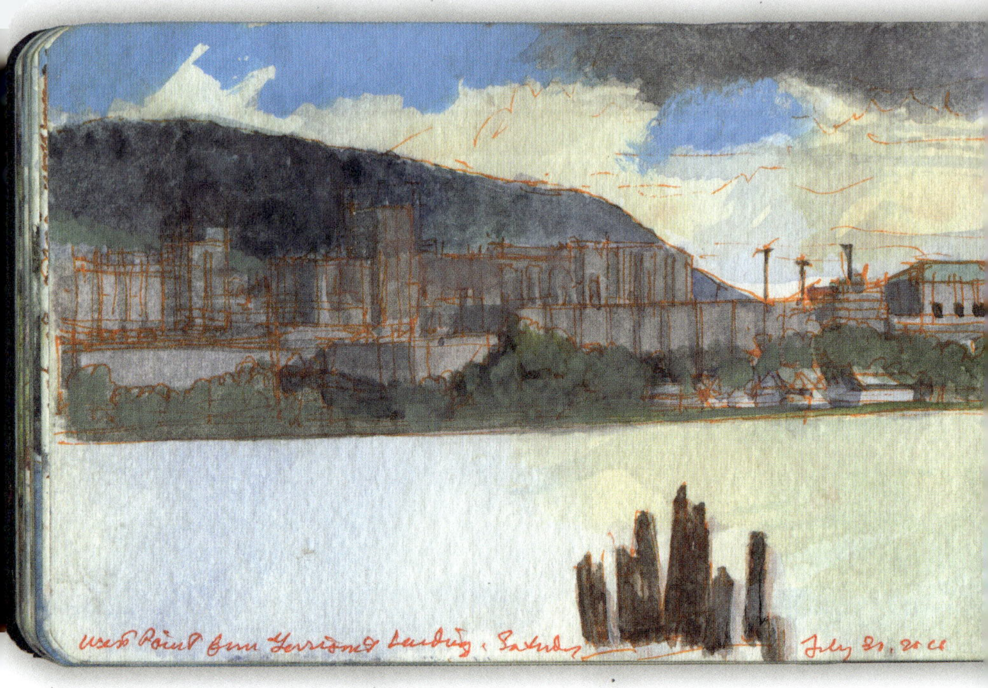

Fig. 1.

WEST POINT FROM GARRISON'S LANDING

When the United States Military Academy at West Point was founded as an engineering school in 1802, the curriculum included topographical drawing and mapmaking. Sylvanus Thayer became superintendent in 1817, expanding the requirement to two hours of daily drawing instruction for second- and third-year cadets. The artwork that launched the Hudson River School was a view of Fort Putnam by Thomas Cole, painted in 1826. West Point quickly became a magnet for artists such as George Catlin, William Bartlett, Benson Lossing, William Guy Wall, John Frederick Kensett, and many others looking for picturesque subjects. Academy graduate and noted ethnographic artist Seth Eastman served as interim head of the drawing academy prior to the

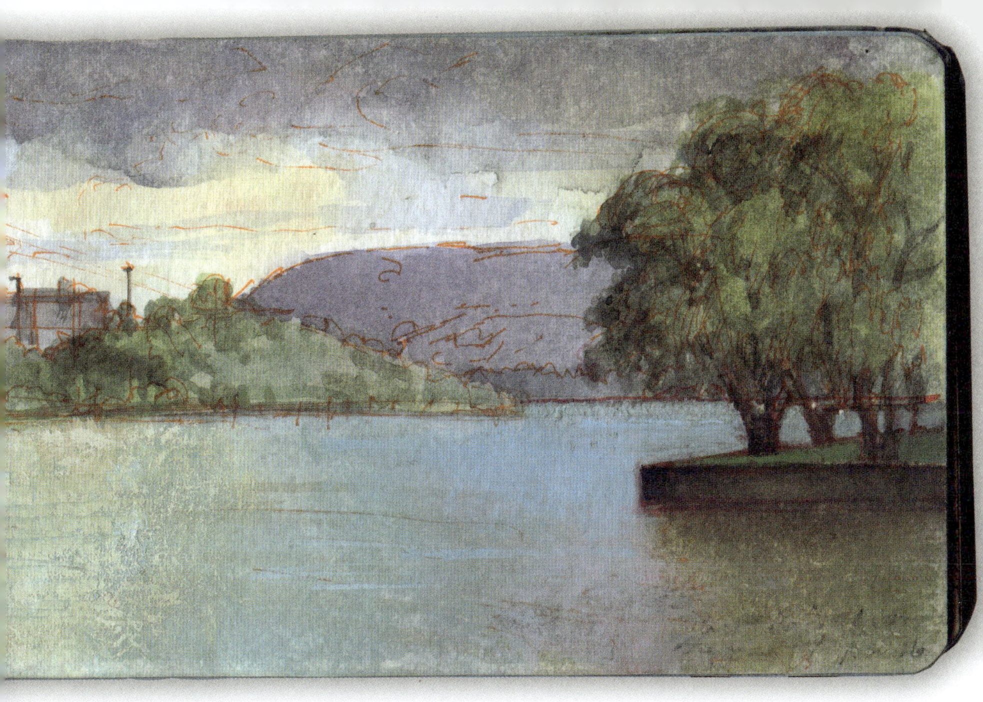

arrival in 1834 of painter Robert W. Weir, whose forty-two-year tenure transformed the program. One of Weir's cadets became the celebrated artist James McNeill Whistler. Rising above the buildings to the left we find Crow's Nest Mountain, which served as a target range for cannon tubes produced at West Point Foundry in Cold Spring, a few miles to the north. A casual observer might fail to realize that what they behold is not just a scenic vista but a key location in American history—a center of science, technology, and art that was to the nineteenth century what Los Alamos was to the 1940s, traversed by a watery thoroughfare.

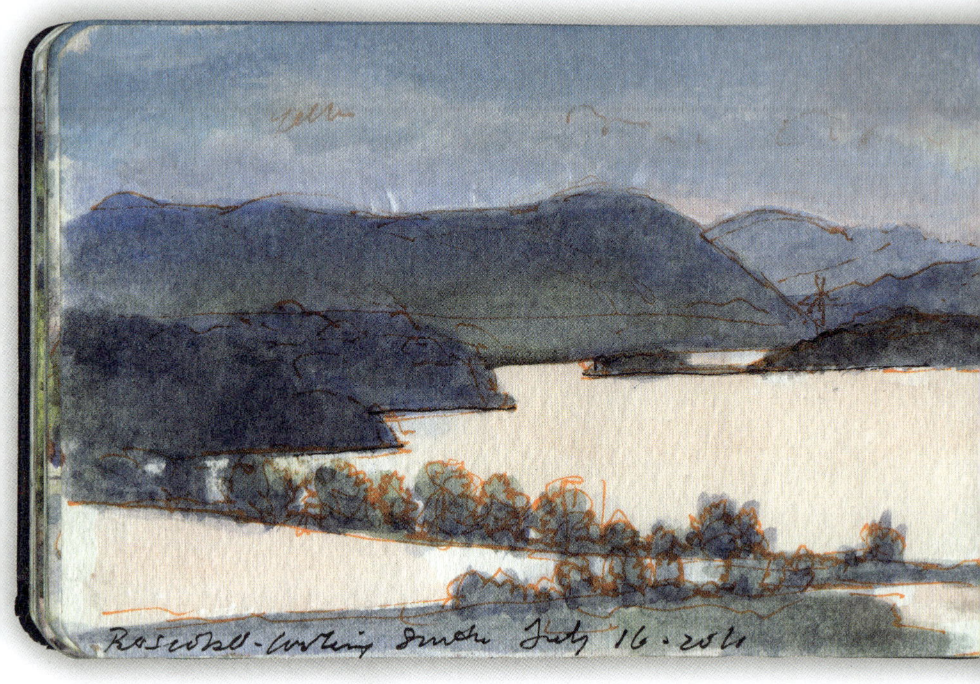

Fig. 2.

LOOKING SOUTH FROM THE BELVEDERE AT BOSCOBEL,

Famed as one of America's scenic treasures, the Hudson Highlands were shaped by the river carving a path through an outcropping of basement rock extending northward from the Reading Prong of Pennsylvania and the Ramapo Mountains of northern New Jersey. The waterway variously known as Muhheahkunnuck, North River, and Hudson's River has been a thoroughfare since the dawn of human habitation. Rising in the Adirondack Mountains, the river flows more than 300 miles (500 kilometers) to its confluence with the Atlantic. In the early nineteenth century, more than three hundred commercial vessels plied the waters daily between Troy and New York City. On September 14, 1608, the *Half-Moon* dropped anchor in these waters. Writing in his journal on September 14, 1609, Robert Juet described the setting.

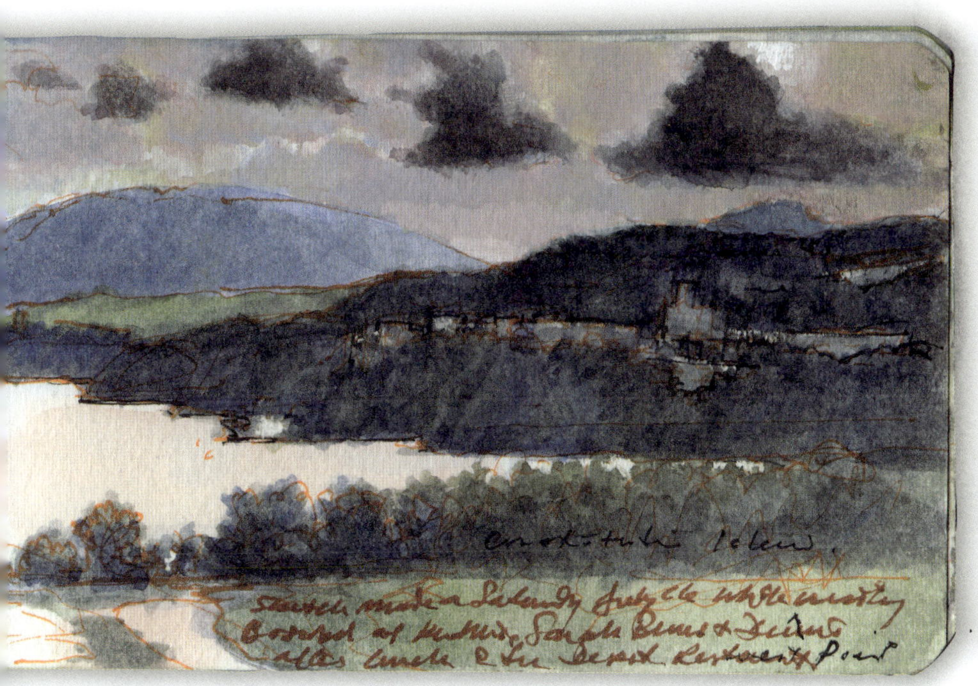

GARRISON, NEW YORK

The Land grew very mountainous. The River is full of fish.

On September 25, 1780, Benedict Arnold boarded the Swan-class war sloop HMS *Vulture* in these very waters. Traversing the foreground is the Hudson Line railway. The marshlands created when the railroad was built in 1851 were briefly converted to rice paddies, but the scheme failed. In the foreground to the right is Constitution Island, with West Point on the far shore. This vista from Boscobel House and Gardens in Garrison, New York, attracts thousands of visitors every year.

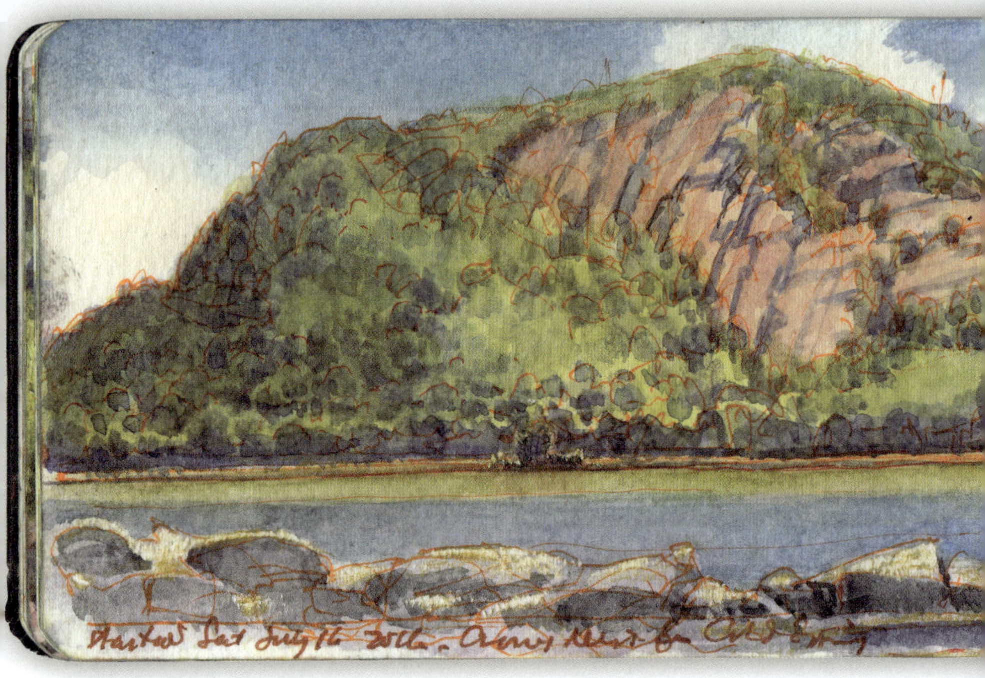

Fig. 3.

CROW'S NEST MOUNTAIN FROM COLD SPRING LANDING

The village of Cold Spring was given its name by George Washington after refreshing himself at a nearby spring. In colonial times, the village was nothing more than a cluster of buildings by a river landing on the estate of Adolphus Philipse. In 1817, Gouverneur Kemble established the West Point Foundry just south of the village. For nearly a century, as the foundry produced artillery pieces for the United States Army, the village grew into a town. Cannon tubes were finished, inspected, and tested by firing live rounds at Crow's Nest Mountain, across the river. The rocky slopes are said to be littered with thousands of cannonballs and unexploded ordnance. The infamous pirate William Kidd is said to have buried his loot at Kidd's Plug,

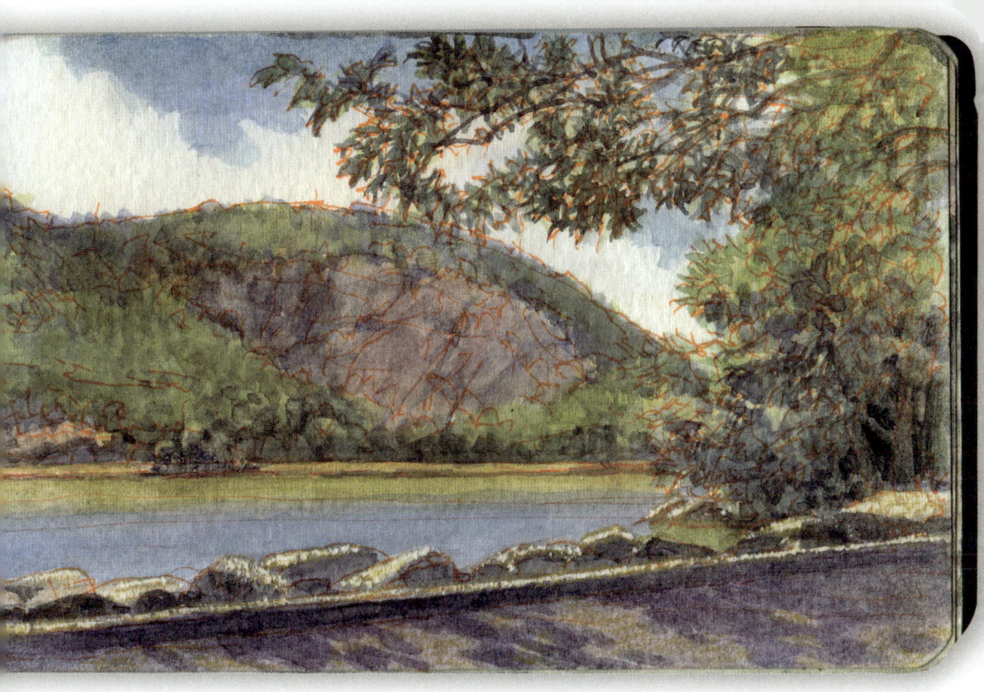

the rocky escarpment at the base of the distant cliffs. Putnam County poet George Pope Morris praised the mountain in verse:

> Where Hudson's waves o'er silvery sands
> Winds through the hills afar,
> And Cro' Nest like a monarch stands
> Crowned with a single star.

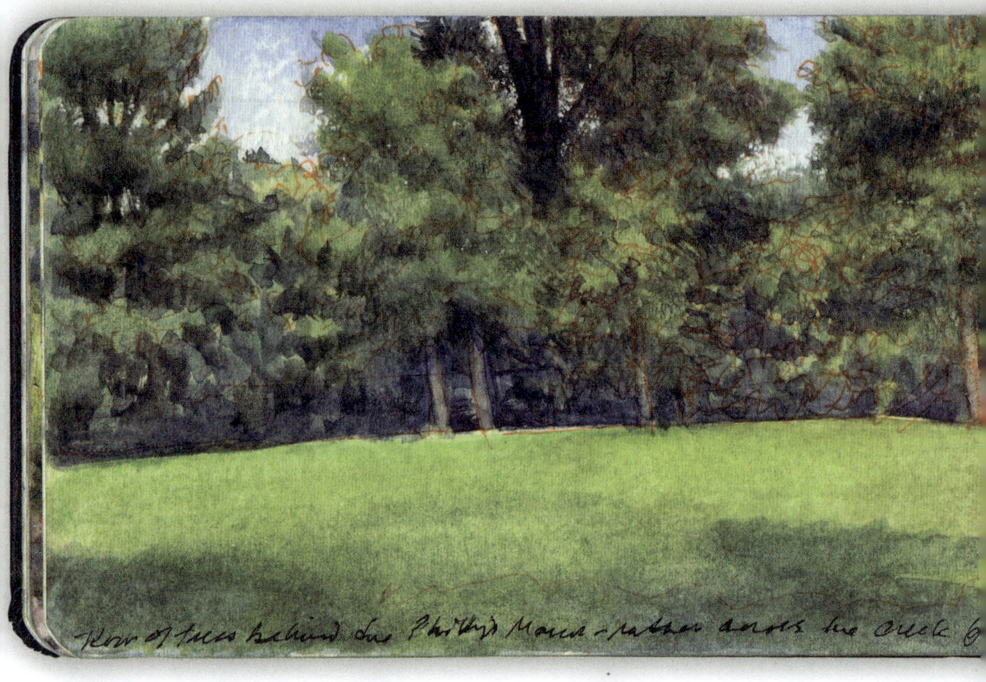

Fig. 4.

A CLEARING NORTH OF PHILIPSE MILLS,

Through the village of Sleepy Hollow, just north of Tarrytown flows a tributary of the Hudson. The Pocantico River feeds a large pond formed by a long, timber-built dam below a narrow bridge with a wooden deck. Its runoff powers a grist-mill that stands at one end of the bridge. Legend, or the imagination of Washington Irving, tells of a lovesick Yankee schoolmaster pursued across the very same bridge, and driven away by a Headless Horseman.

The mill, the land, and much of Westchester County were once owned by the Philipse family. Loyalists during the Revolutionary War, they were stripped of their property and fled to Britain.

The site today is a national historic landmark. From the gift shop of Philipse

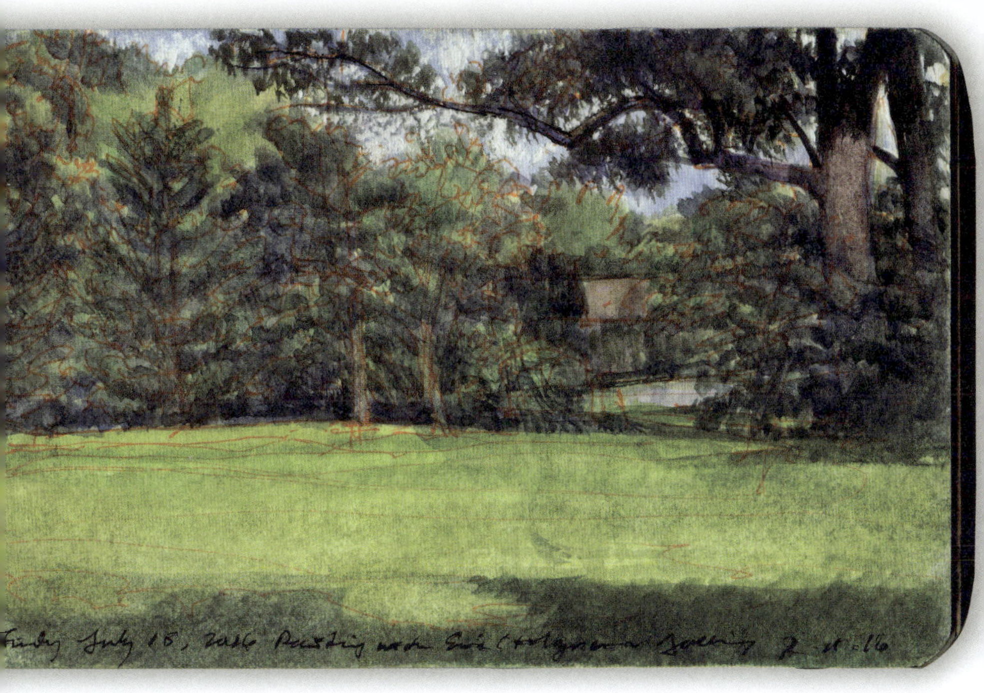

SLEEPY HOLLOW, NEW YORK

Manor, bus tours bring visitors to Kykuit, the estate of the late New York governor Nelson Aldrich Rockefeller. Eric Holzman is a wonderful painter and a friend for fifty years. Growing up in Yonkers, Ric knew all the river towns opposite the Palisades and north along Tappan Zee. One day we drove to Sleepy Hollow. Enthralled by otherworldly vine-strangled trees, Eric positioned his easel behind a screen of vegetation along Gory Brook. Walking through a stand of trees, I settled on a spot at the far end of a small field. We took breaks, exchanged critiques. Such days are forever.

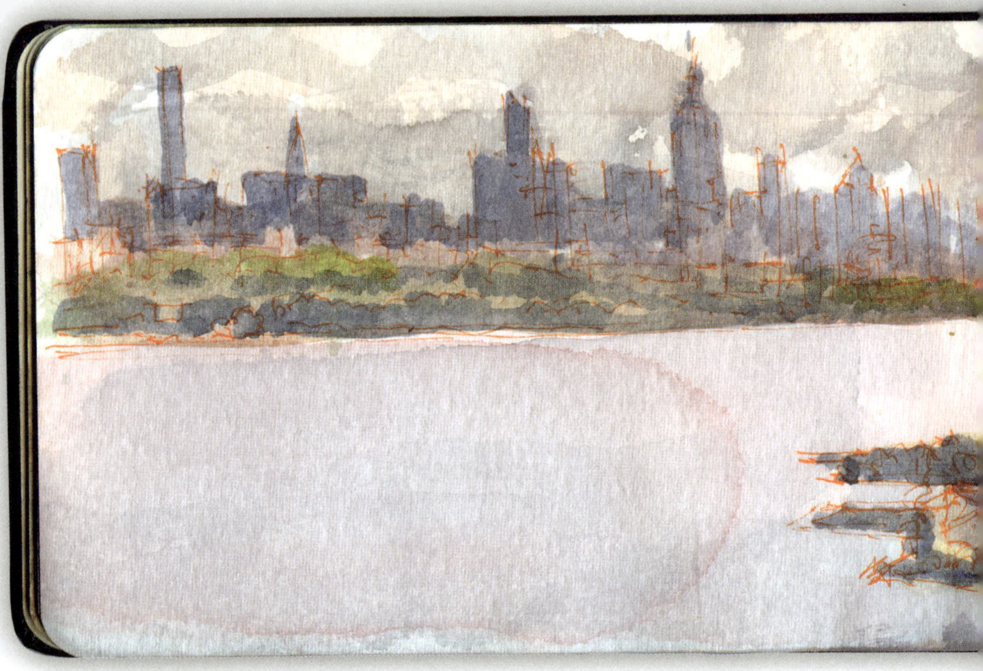

Fig. 5.

MANHATTAN FROM FORT LEE

The Lenni-Lenape called the Palisades Weehawken: rocks that look like trees. On a grassy ledge, just north of the western portal of the Lincoln Tunnel, Vice President Aaron Burr mortally wounded former secretary of the treasury Alexander Hamilton in a duel fought on July 11, 1804. The site is 6 miles downstream from this overlook. The southern end of Fort Lee State Park is marked by a steep declivity, a break in the sheer precipice that girds the western bank of the river. Across the Hudson River, northern Manhattan landmarks like Riverside Church and Grant's Tomb are visible, with the towers of Midtown and Lower Manhattan beyond. Pairs of fit Asian women walked and jogged along the park trail behind where I was painting.

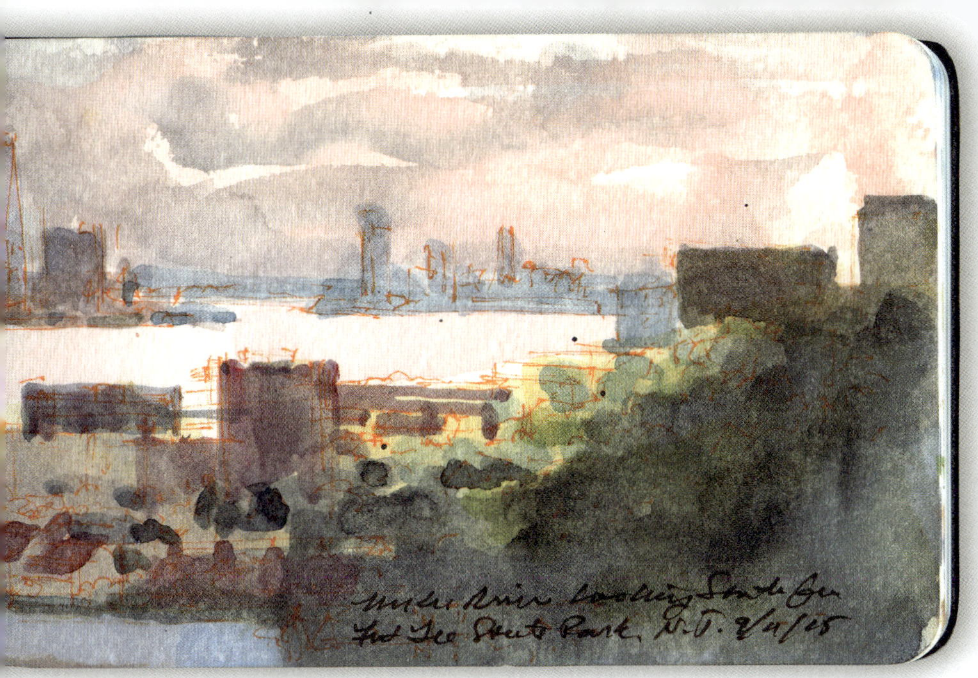

One stopped and asked if I was married. “Yes,” I replied, just before she disappeared.

A century earlier, Fort Lee had become a major center of motion picture production. William Fox established Fox Film Corporation in 1915. Young Thomas Hart Benton worked in Fort Lee as a scenic artist. Film crews shot cliffhanger endings along the Palisades, for serials like *The Perils of Pauline*. Despite the sylvan setting, there was a constant roar from the bridge. Clouds rolled in from the west. A soft rain threw the distant skyline out of focus.

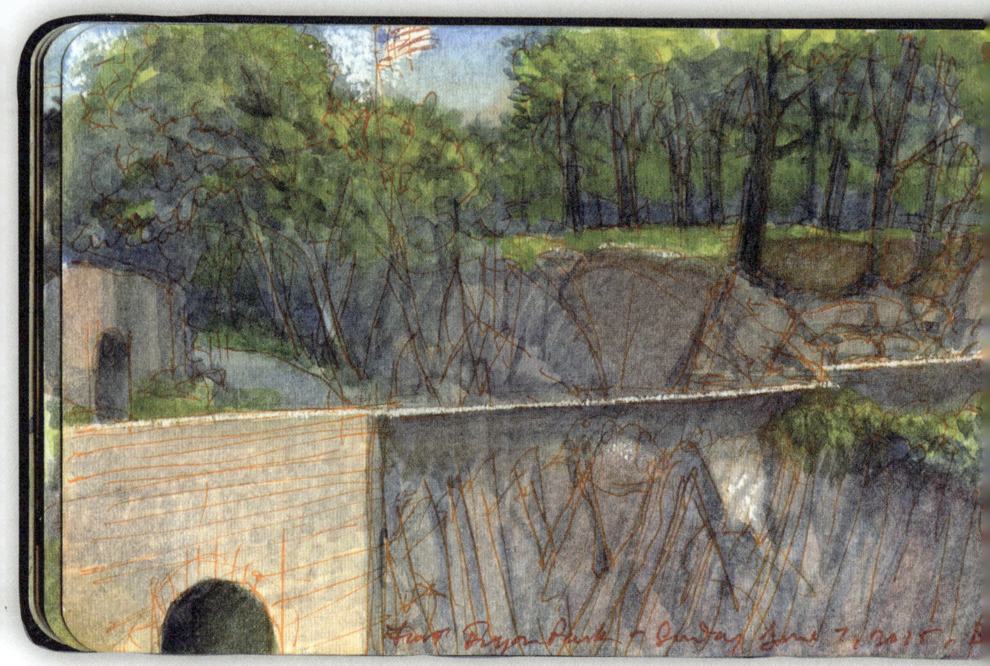

Fig. 6.

FORT TRYON PARK, NORTHERN MANHATTAN

Posted behind hilltop breastworks high above the river, Continental artillerists were overwhelmed by Hessian infantry. One of the gunners was killed. His young wife fought in his stead until she fell wounded. The captured Patriot redoubt was renamed Fort Tryon, in honor of the Royal Governor of New York. Permanently disabled, Margaret Corbin survived for another quarter century. Marking the sheer eastern face of the rocky hill upon which Corbin had fought is a large bronze plaque, placed there to honor her sacrifice

During the 1930s, newly constructed gardens, paths, and stairways transformed the former battlefield into a park. Corbin's stand lies buried under

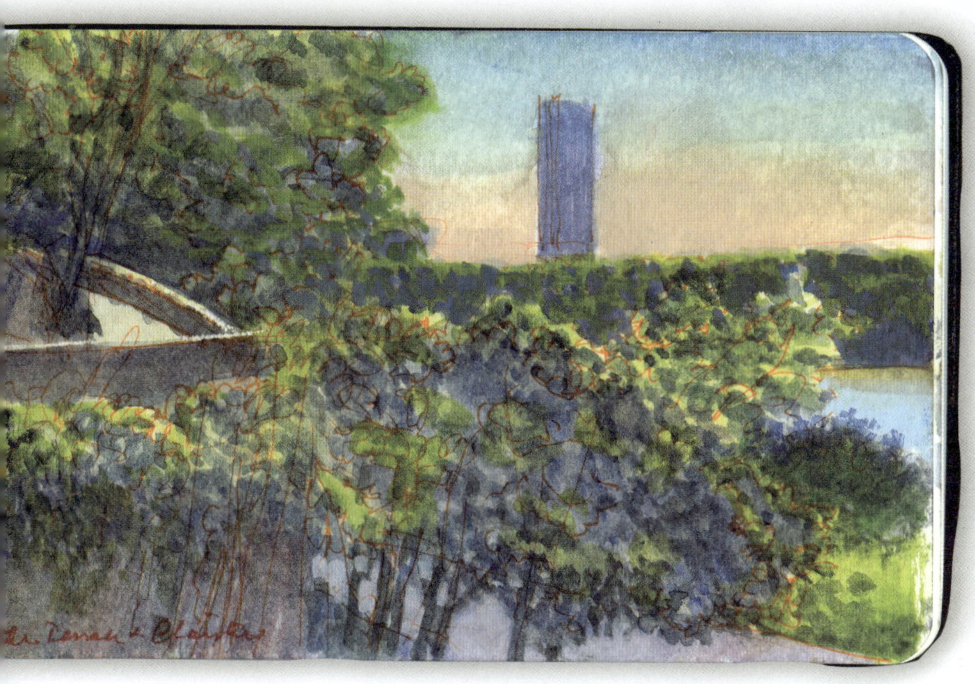

masonry terraces, evoking a historic fortification. Day and night, the national colors fly at its summit. In the midnineties, celebrities like Bette Midler and Washington Heights resident Dr. Ruth Westheimer helped transform the park into one of the most beautiful in the city, and one of the least crowded. At the northern end of the park stands a cluster of reconstructed European chapels and gardens. Resting my sketchbook atop a stone wall, people drifted by me as I painted. No one paused to look over my shoulder. This is New York. When film stars, world leaders, or raving lunatics stroll down the avenue, nobody gives them a second look.

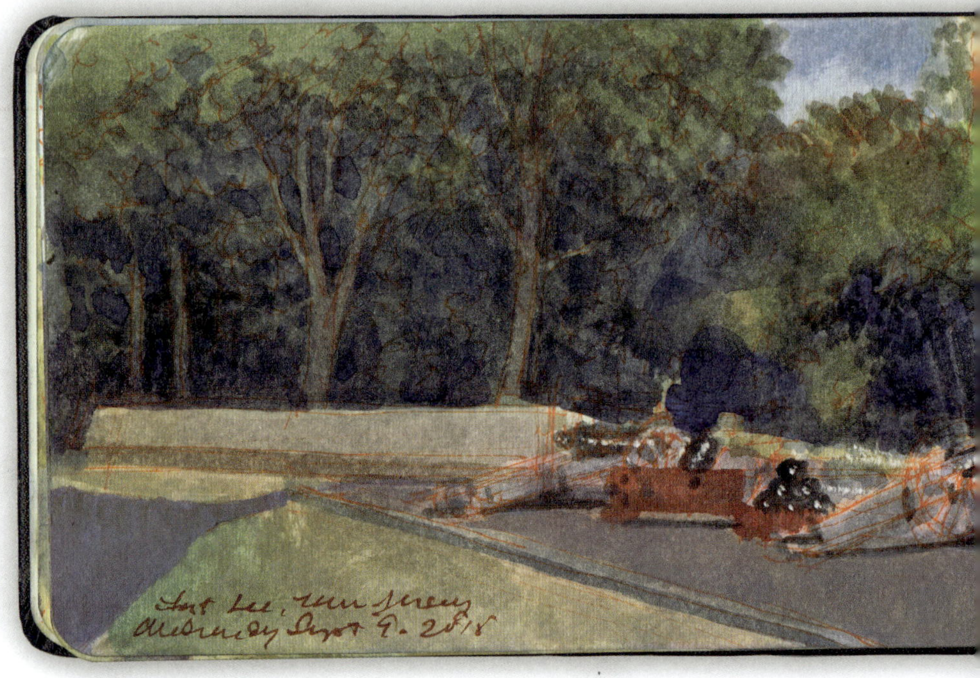

Fig. 7.

REVOLUTIONARY WAR BATTERY, FORT LEE, NEW JERSEY

From Fort Lee atop the Jersey Palisades, George Washington watched in horror on November 16, 1776, as British and Hessian troops overwhelmed Continentals who had taken cover in Fort Washington, a large earthwork occupying the highest point on the island of Manhattan.

Shortly thereafter, Redcoats led by Charles Cornwallis scaled the Palisades a few miles to the north, intending to trap Washington with a flank attack. Washington instead executed a brilliant withdrawal across New Jersey and into Bucks County, Pennsylvania. Five weeks later he crossed the Delaware and fell on the Hessian garrison at Trenton, winning a stunning victory for the Patriot cause.

Construction of the George Washington Bridge, which opened in 1932, carved

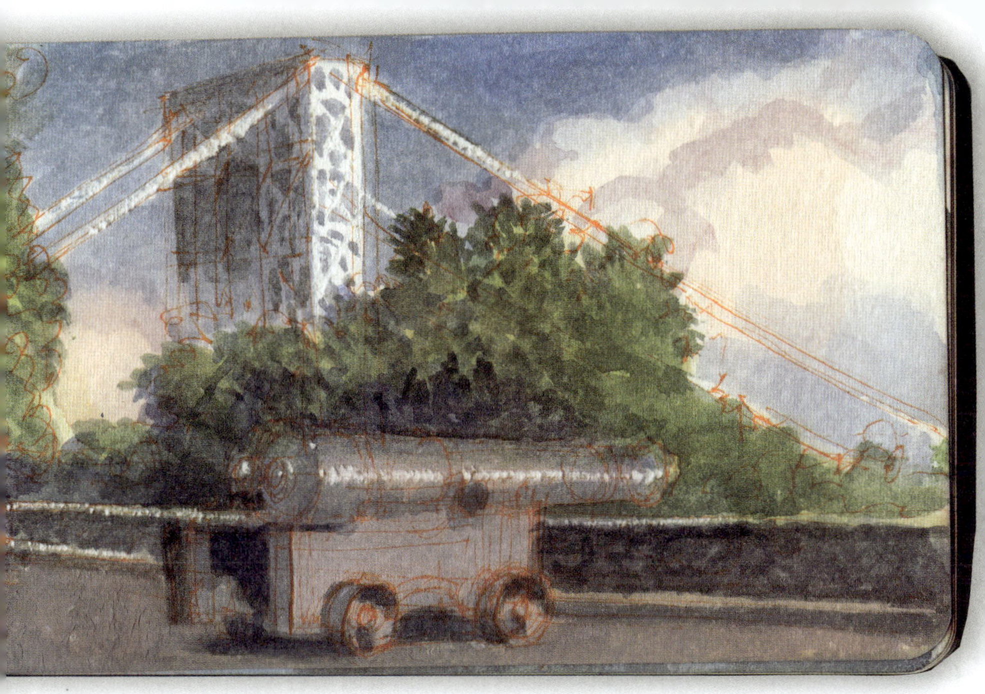

a ditch through the basaltic diabase cliffs to accommodate the roadway. In 1937, New York and New Jersey created the Palisades Interstate Park Commission, with Monument Park (Fort Lee) as its southernmost terminus. For the bicentennial of the American Revolution, parking lots and an interpretive center were built. Earthworks were restored to re-create the feeling of an eighteenth-century fort. When I first visited the site in the nineties, fiberglass revetments had faded and were cracking. Recent improvements replaced these with timbers. A blockhouse and cabin were built, along with a coastal battery. On the anniversary of the battle, reenactor artillerymen fire salutes from the cannons, rattling Manhattan windowpanes.

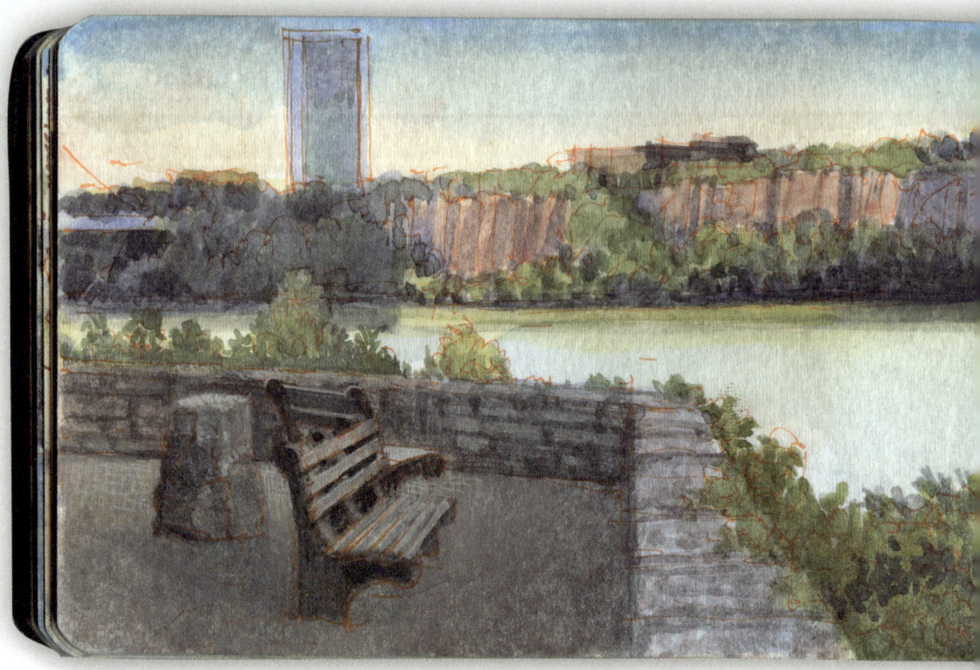

Fig. 8.

THE JERSEY PALISADES FROM BELOW THE CLOISTERS

Shaded by rocky outcroppings, an esplanade runs along the bluff, offering spectacular views of the Jersey Palisades—a sheer wall of basaltic diabase sill. A hundred yards to the southeast of this prospect stands the Cloisters—a facility operated by the Metropolitan Museum of Art as a museum of medieval art. Comprised of reconstructed enclosures, gardens, and chapels collected by sculptor George Grey Barnard that later were acquired by John D. Rockefeller Jr. and reassembled atop North Hill in Washington Heights by architect Charles Collens, the site was previously occupied by an estate owned by industrialist, harness-racing enthusiast, and art collector Cornelius Billings. Known today as Fort Tryon Park, rocky vertiginous terrain is

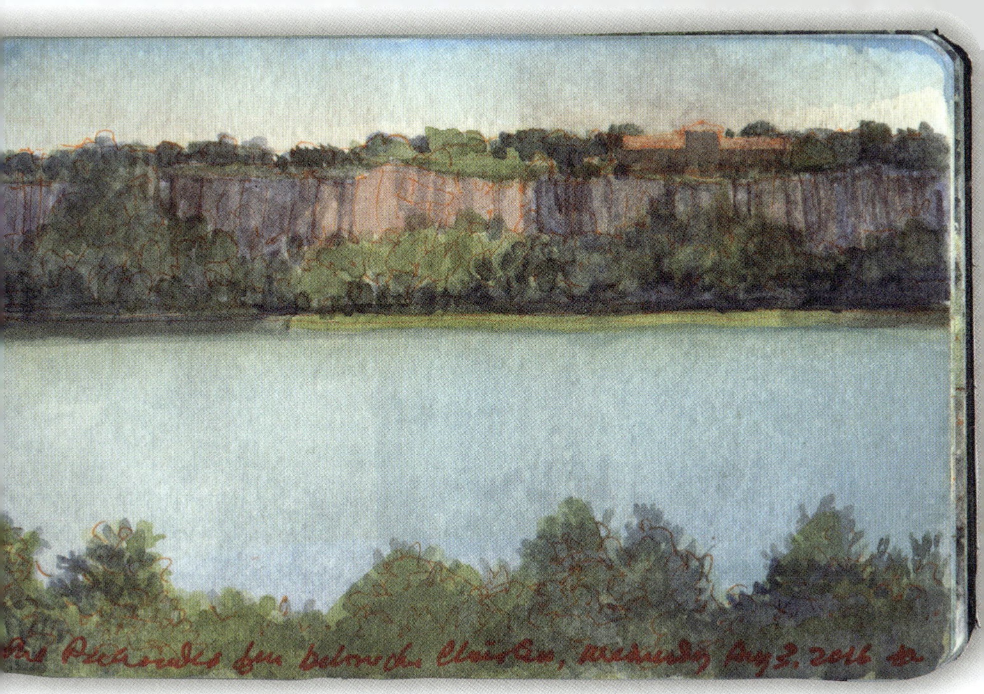

crisscrossed by stairways, trails, woodlands, and clearings laid out by Frederick Law Olmsted Jr. Trails descend to Broadway and Dyckman Avenue, where pedestrians and bicyclists can access a trail that leads downstream to the Battery. This view is from a ledge on the northwestern shoulder of North Hill, near the advance of Hessians led by Johann Rall, on November 16, 1776. Wildlife has returned to the park. Visiting the park, I have beheld avian species, including bald eagles, as well as woodchucks, skunks, raccoons, and worrisome reptiles.

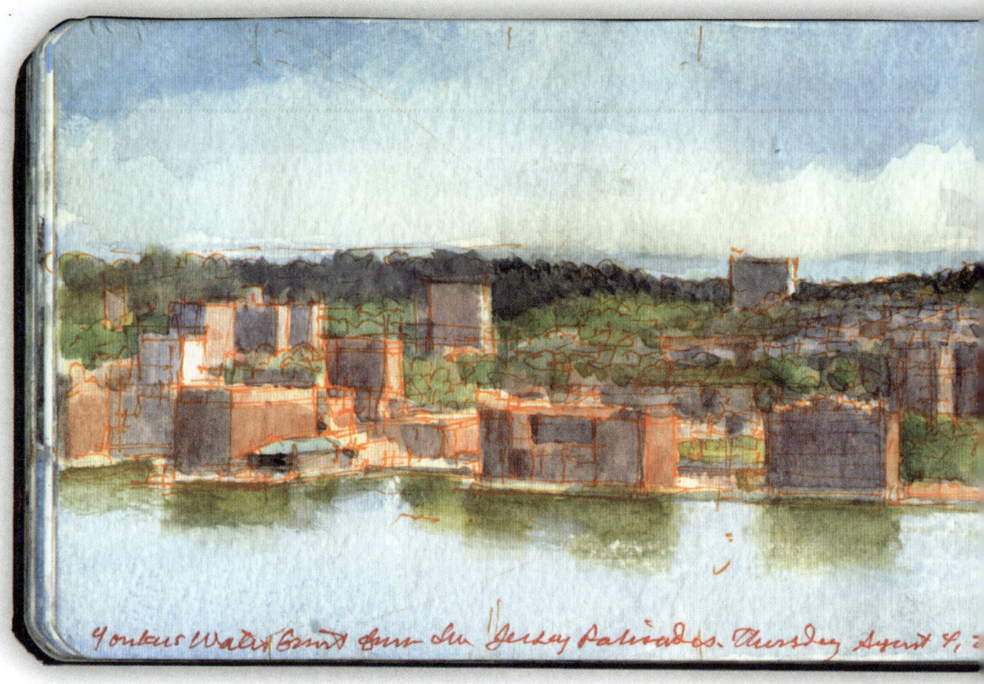

Fig. 9.

YONKERS FROM THE LONG PATH

Stretching between the 175th Street bus station, located at the eastern end of the George Washington Bridge, the Long Path follows historic trails connecting the New Jersey Palisades with the northern Helderberg Mountains west of Albany. Part of the new 700-mile Empire State Trail system, at its southern end the Long Path follows the rim of the Palisades, in the wooded margins between the precipice and Palisades Interstate Parkway. Debouching here and there at scenic parking areas along the motorway, the trail offers stunning vistas of the Bronx and Westchester County. Alpine scenic overlook lies directly across the river from downtown Yonkers. Established in 1645, a sawmill was built near the mouth of Nepperhan Creek, on land held by the Jonkheer (young lord) local patroon Adriaen van der Donck.

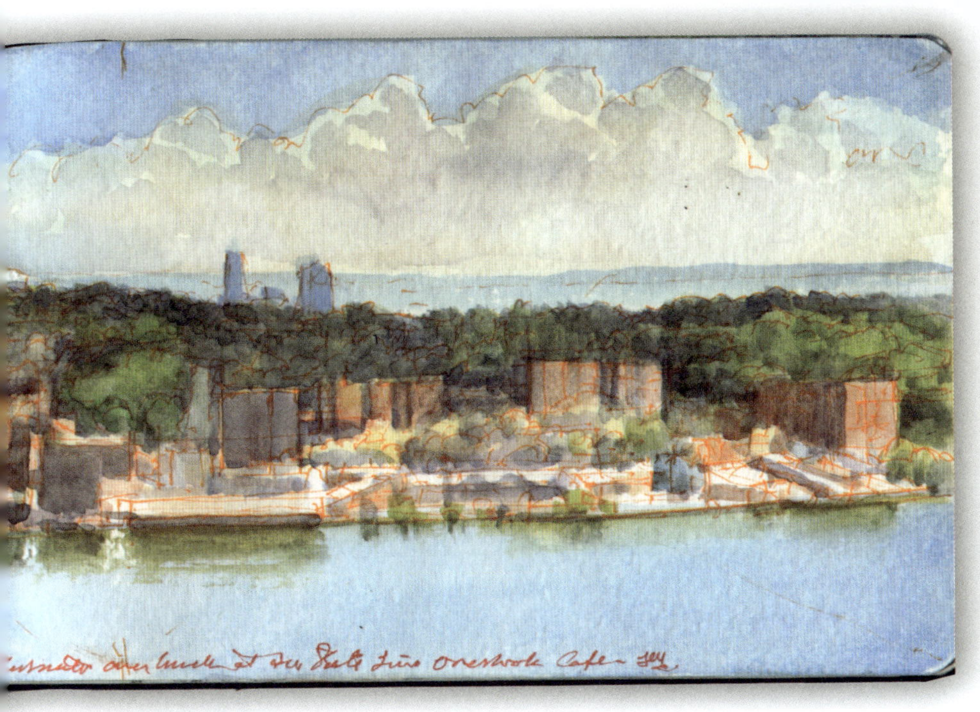

The village soon grew up around the mill's river landing, which came to be known as Jonkheers, or Yonkers. During the nineteenth century the town grew into an industrial center, producing goods from firearms to elevators, carpets, and Bakelite. Access to both river and rail traffic, the small city prospered. The nation's first golf course opened in Yonkers. The decline of local industry and a rise in racial tension troubled Yonkers in the last century but the city is enjoying a renewal, with the redevelopment of the waterfront and other improvements. The Hudson River Museum and Planetarium is located in Trevor Park, in the Glenwood section of northern Yonkers. Seen from a grassy slope below the parking area, the bluffs of Long Island rim the horizon, past the towers of Coop City on the shores of Pelham Bay.

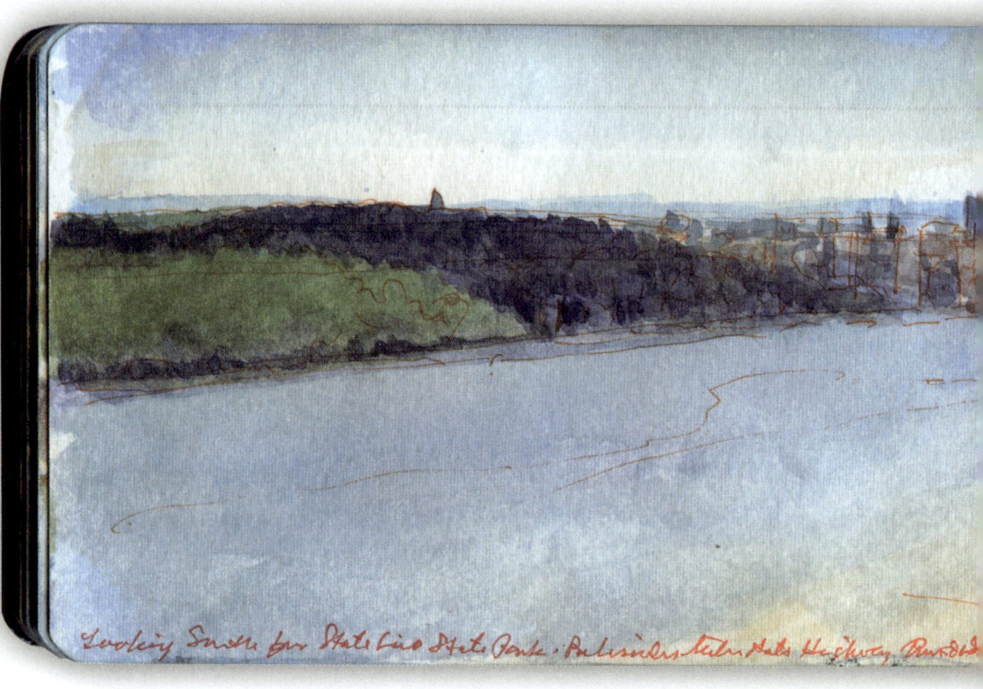

Fig. 10.

YONKERS FROM STATE LINE PARK

The Palisades Interstate Park Commission was created in 1900, by a mutual agreement between the states of New York and New Jersey to preserve the natural environment on the right bank of the Hudson River, and to protect the Palisades from being quarried like Hook Mountain, an extension of the same basaltic sill that rises up from the northwestern shores of Tappan Zee. Parklands atop the Palisades are traversed by the Long Path—a historic trail, now part of the Empire State Trail. A short distance south of the boundary line between the two states the trail reaches State Line Overlook, which is also accessible from the northbound lanes of the Palisades Interstate Parkway. A large parking lot serves the café, visitor center, and bookstore. The path

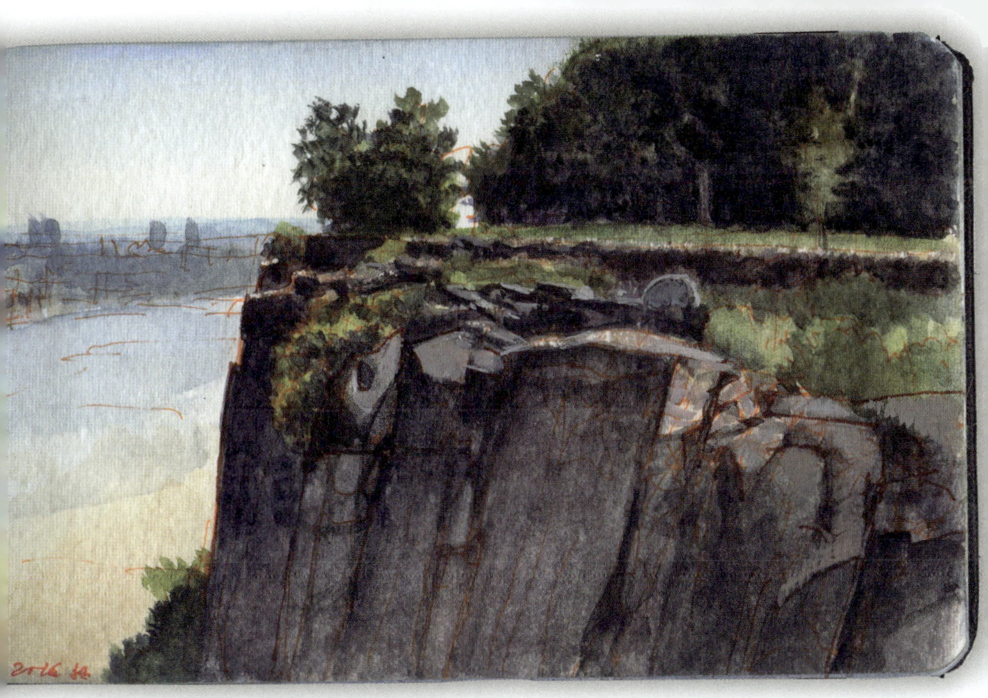

at this point is macadamized. Several walled promontories have been built at the very edge of the cliffs. Looking north across the river one finds the village of Hastings-on-Hudson, with Dobbs Ferry beyond. To the south are wooded hills occupied by Lenoir Preserve, Untermeyer Gardens, and Trevor Park. Beyond, the warm tones masonry and tall buildings mark the location of downtown Yonkers. Taking note of the number of passing ships and oil barges, I tried to envision the Hudson in 1820, with a quotidian flotilla of several hundred steamboats and sailing vessels plying its waters, a major artery of trade and empire.

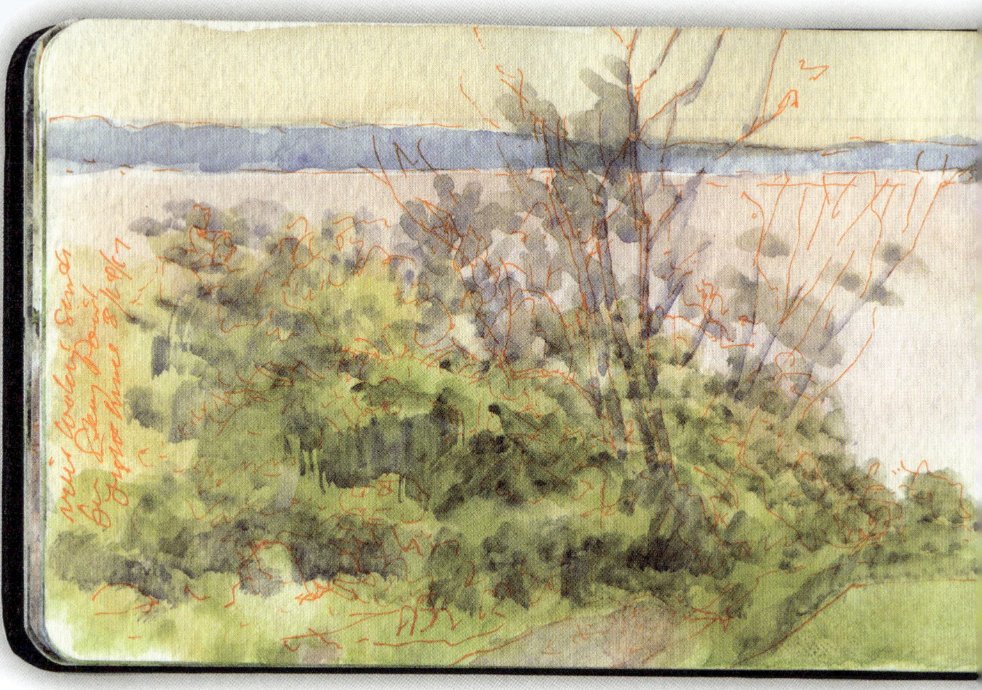

Fig. 11.

HOOK MOUNTAIN AND THE TORS SEEN FROM

On July 16, 1779 General (Mad) Anthony Wayne led a night assault against a British garrison stationed on a rocky promontory on the right bank of the Hudson. Reaching across the river toward Verplanck's Point on the eastern bank of the river, Stony Point marks the division between Haverstraw Bay and the southern waters of Peekskill Bay. Wading through waist-deep water in a soggy marsh, Wayne's troops silently scaled the precipitous bluffs, taking the redcoats by surprise. Looking from one of the fortified positions, Hook Mountain and the Tors rise up along the southern horizon. A few miles north of the heights, Treason Creek flows into the Hudson. Along its banks near the confluence, Benedict Arnold had delivered to Major John Andre plans

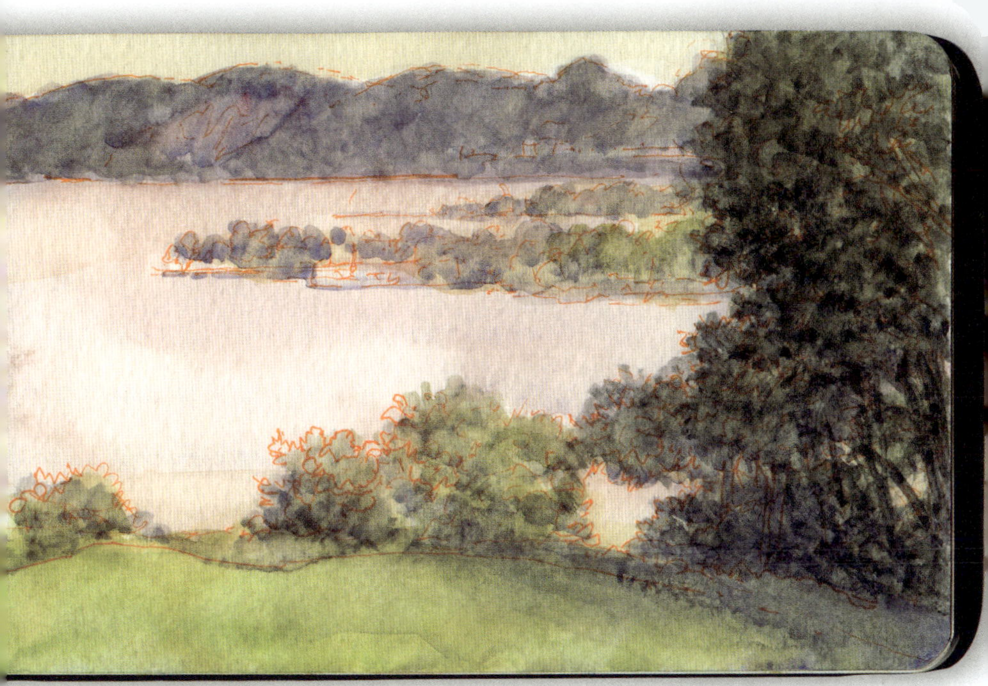

STONY POINT

of the American fortifications at West Point. The site today is a state historic site, interpreting the Revolutionary period and the 1779 battle. The house where Arnold plotted treason is gone. The hill upon which it stood is occupied by Helen Hayes Memorial Hospital. Hook Mountain and the Tors are preserved as part of the Palisades Interstate Park, with hiking trails, lakes, and other recreational amenities.

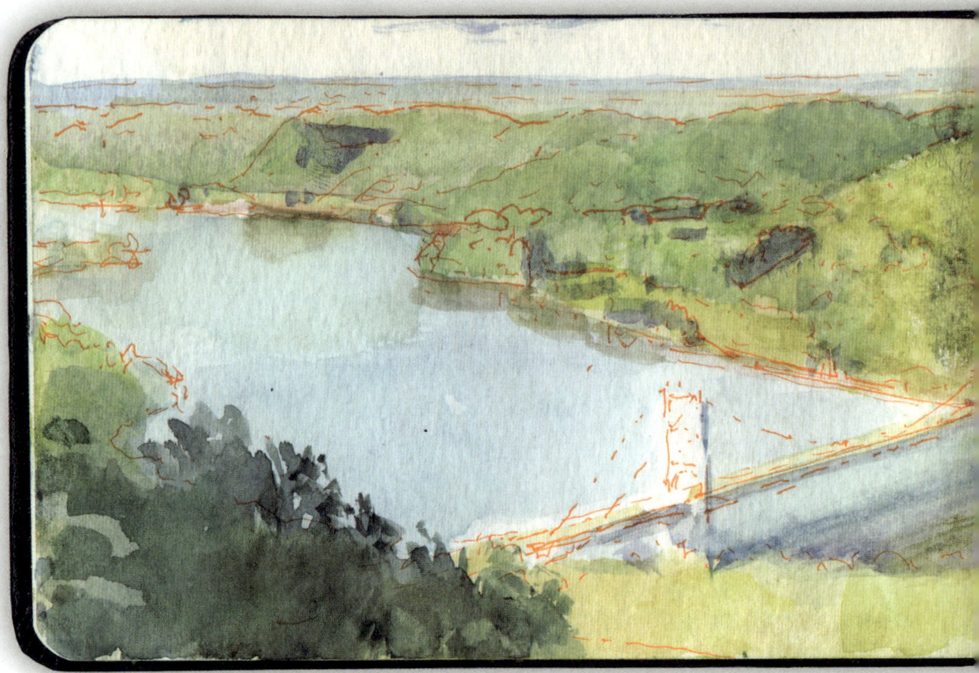

Fig. 12.

ANTHONY'S NOSE SEEN FROM BEAR MOUNTAIN

According to Washington Irving, the crew of *Half-Moon,* or perhaps to its captain Henry Hudson, this rocky promontory resembled the allegedly bulbous proboscis of the trumpeter, Anthony von Corlaer. Robert Juet's journal of the voyage illuminates nothing about Anthony's character, or even his appearance. Name origin myths abound, such as sea captain Anthony Hogan whose nose was said to rival Cyrano. Whatever the truth may be, the name had made its appearance on legal documents by the late seventeenth century. During the Revolutionary War, patriot forces established twin forts across the river, on opposing bluffs above the mouth of Popolopen Creek. To impede enemy warships, a stout chain of giant iron links was stretched across the river, laid upon a series of rafts between Fort Montgomery

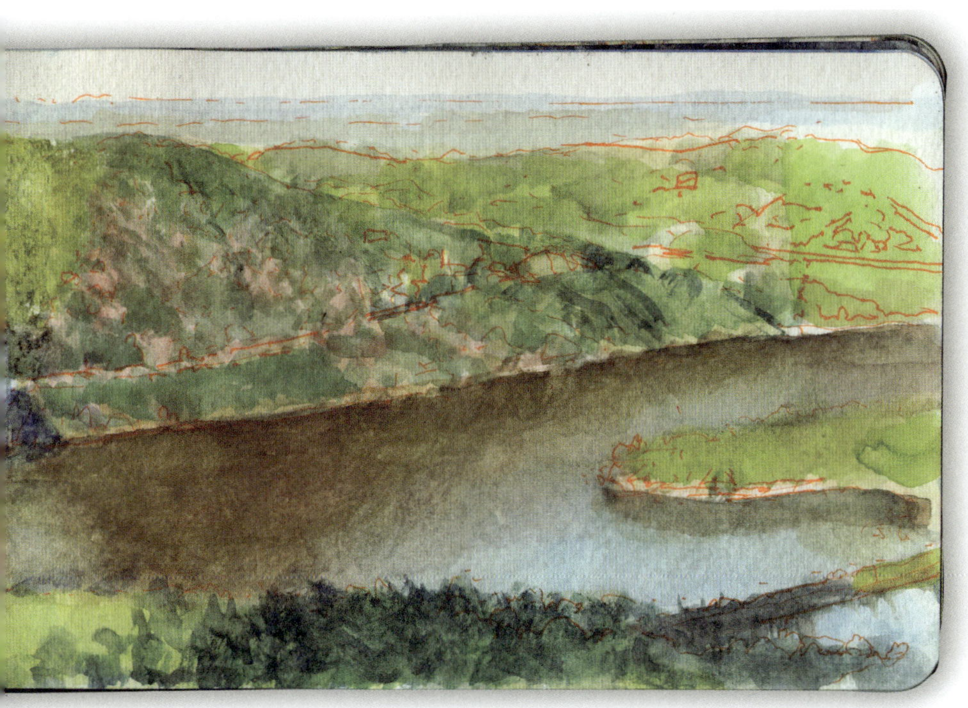

to the north, and the western base of Anthony's Nose to the east. On October 6, 1777, a combined force of Crown forces marched from Stony Point behind Thunder Hill and Bear Mountain, capturing the forts and dismantling the chain. The first section of the Appalachian Trail opened here in 1923, stretching southward across Harriman State Park. In 1924 private interests began construction of Bear Mountain Bridge. For a short time, it held the record as the longest suspension bridge in the world. To the south is Iona Island. A few miles to the north is the village of Highland Falls, adjoining the US Military Academy at West Point. Less than an hour's train ride from Grand Central Terminal, the Hudson Highlands region has been called "America's Rhineland."

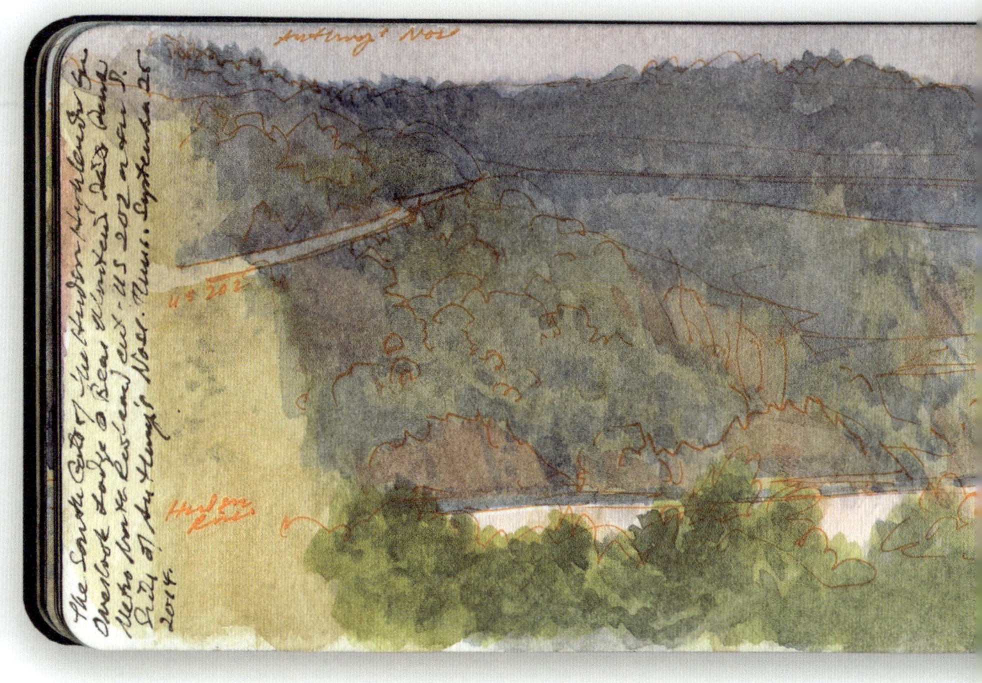

Fig. 13.

SOUTH GATE FROM BEAR MOUNTAIN

Bending around Trophy Point, the river follows a straight course for several miles, passing Buttermilk Falls and a small island known as Con Hook below the guns of Fort Montgomery on a bluff just north of where Popolopen Creek spills into the Hudson. It was here that American patriot forces stretched a heavy iron chain floating on a series of rafts across the river, below the mountain known as Anthony's Nose. Connecting its vertiginous western face to Fort Clinton—Montgomery's twin—on the bluff south of Popolopen Creek is Bear Mountain Bridge. Here the banks of the river widen again. A railway runs along a levee, enclosing an arm of the river that has become marshland over the years. The tracks cross Iona Island, which served as a

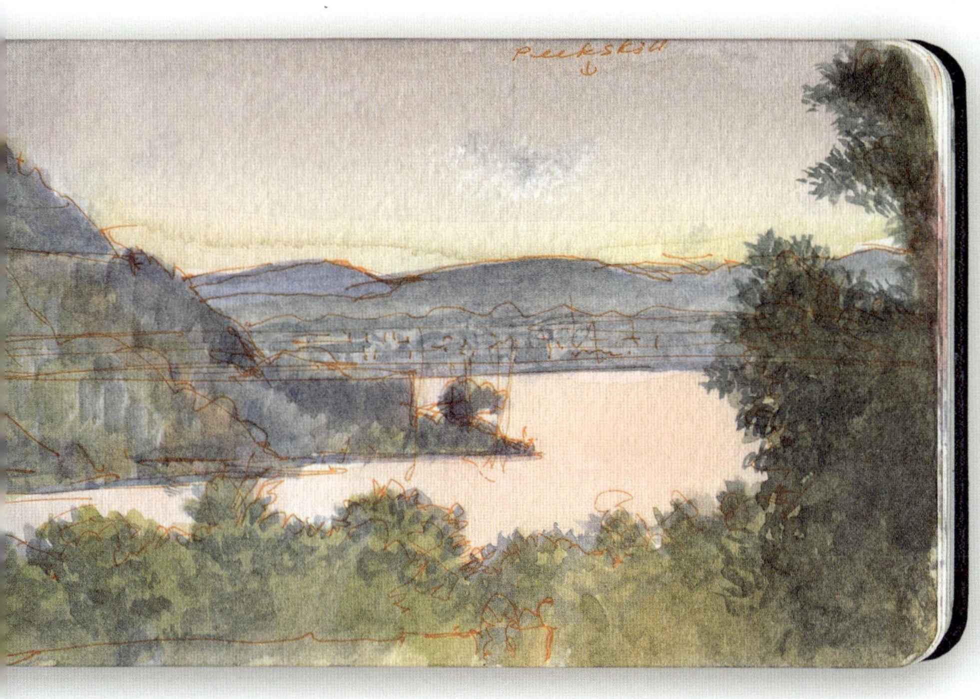

naval weapons depot during the twentieth century. Parts of the rocky islet remain off limits to the public. To the south, reaching eastward, is Dunderberg Mountain, or Thunder Hill, the downriver side of the south gate to the Hudson Highlands. Forming the northern gatepost is Roa Hook, below the southern declivity of Anthony's Nose. Cast in shadow, a small concrete structure marks the location in this painting. The view is from the deck of Bear Mountain Inn's Overlook Lodge, looking southeast toward the city of Peekskill, across the bay that bears its name.

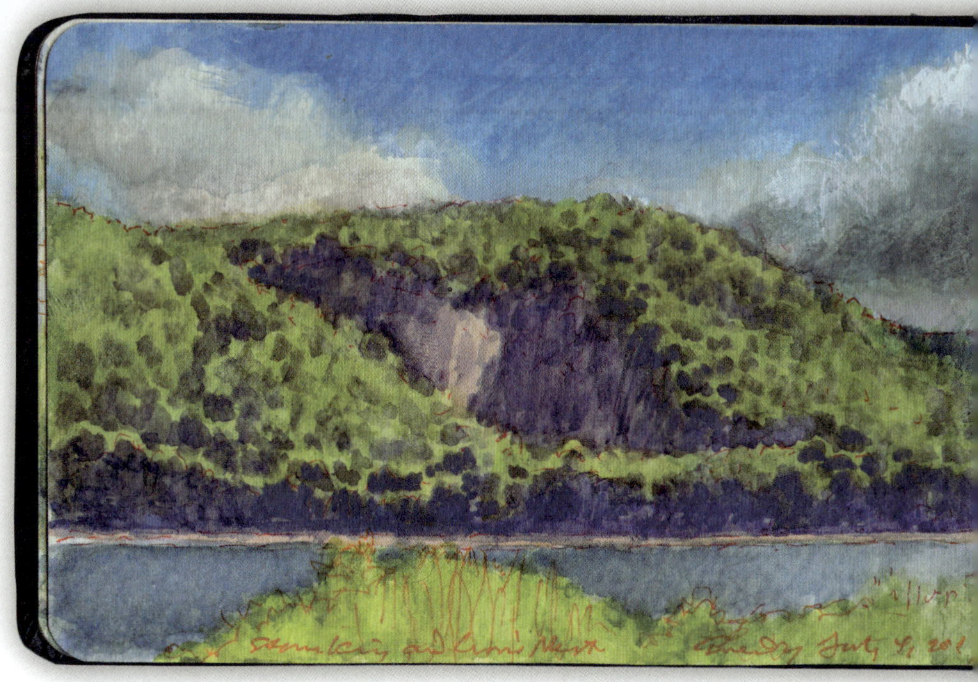

Fig. 14.

STORM KING FROM COLD SPRING VILLAGE

The Dutch named Boterberg (Butter Hill), the mountain on the right, because it resembled a butter loaf. Rising more than 1,300 feet above the river, Butter Hill is formed of Proterozoic granite and gneiss distorted by plate tectonics. Its present form was sculpted between 100,000 and 120,000 years ago by glaciation that sheared off its southern slope to expose the rock face visible today. The Hudson Highlands ranks as one of America's two fjords. The other, Somes Sound at Mount Desert Island in Maine, is where I first witnessed similar evidence of glacial activity smoothing one side of a geological uplift and tumbling down the other. Taking up residence north of Butter Hill, poet and critic Nathaniel Parker Willis named his hilltop estate Idlewild.

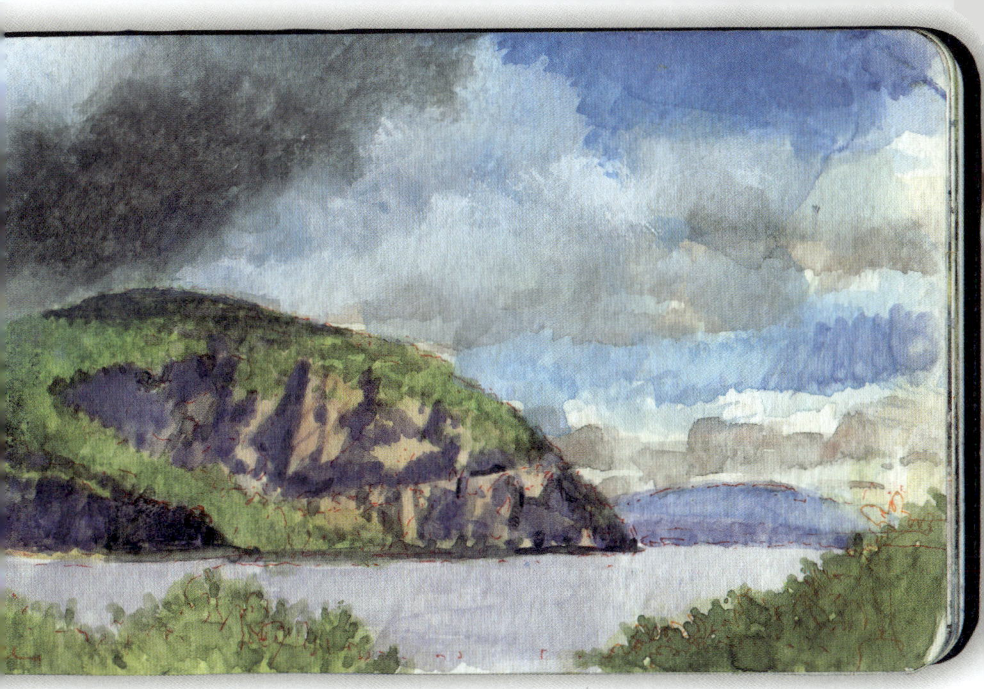

In an age when explorers crisscrossed the globe naming every rock, tree, and puddle, Butter Hill did not sit well with Willis, who, in today's parlance, gave it a better brand.

> "Standing aloft before other mountains in the chain, this sign is peculiar to him. He seems the monarch, and this seems his stately ordering of a change in the weather. Should not STORM-KING, then, be his proper title?"

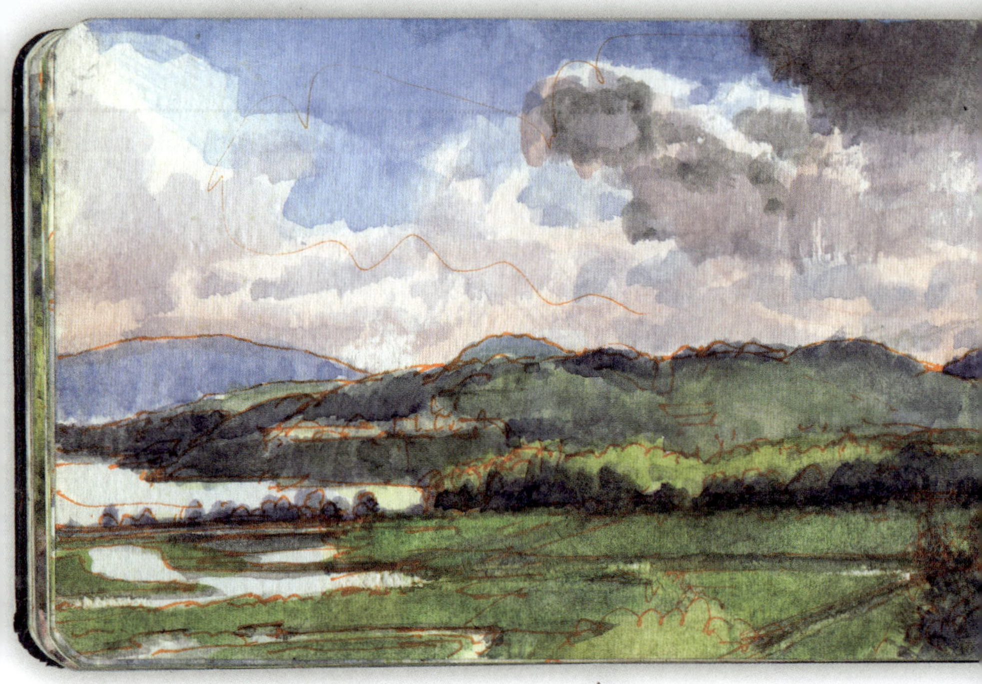

Fig. 15.

WESTERN HIGHLANDS FROM BOSCOBEL

To the southwest, the orderly divisions of Constitution Marsh become apparent. Channels were cut through the marshland during the second quarter of the nineteenth century for the cultivation of wild rice. The blue summit at left is Bear Mountain. The gray dashes in the foliage above the river are the stone buildings of West Point. Enclosed by the Hudson Line causeway to the right is Foundry Cove, which is fed by Indian Brook. By the late twentieth century, industrial waste had resulted in the Hudson having the greatest concentration of cadmium pollution on the planet. Folk singer and activist Pete Seeger conceived the idea of building a replica nineteenth-century gaff-rigged sloop and offering cruises and concerts to promote the

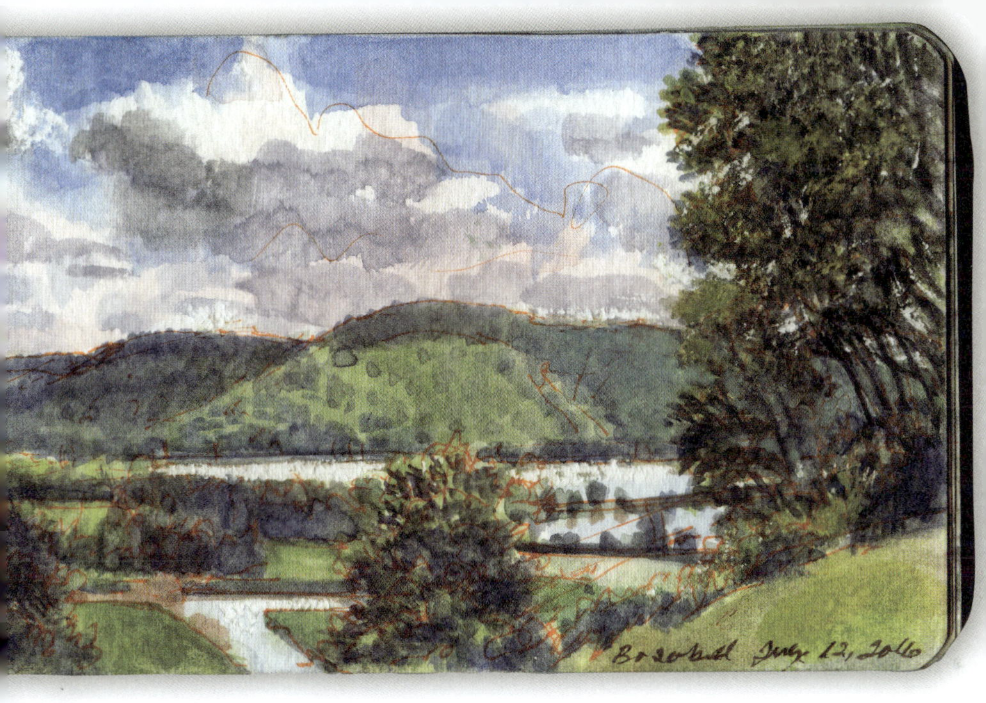

rehabilitation of the Hudson Estuary. Public outcry led Consolidated Edison to abandon plans for a massive hydroelectric facility that would have cut into the north slope of Storm King Mountain, several miles upriver. The land is now a state park. Constitution Marsh is today a wildlife refuge, providing habitat for local waterfowl such as herons and egrets as well as a number of songbirds, migratory birds, and bald eagles. Every June, almost one thousand snapping turtles come out of the marsh to lay their eggs. More than forty years later the sloop Clearwater continues to carry Seeger's message up and down the river.

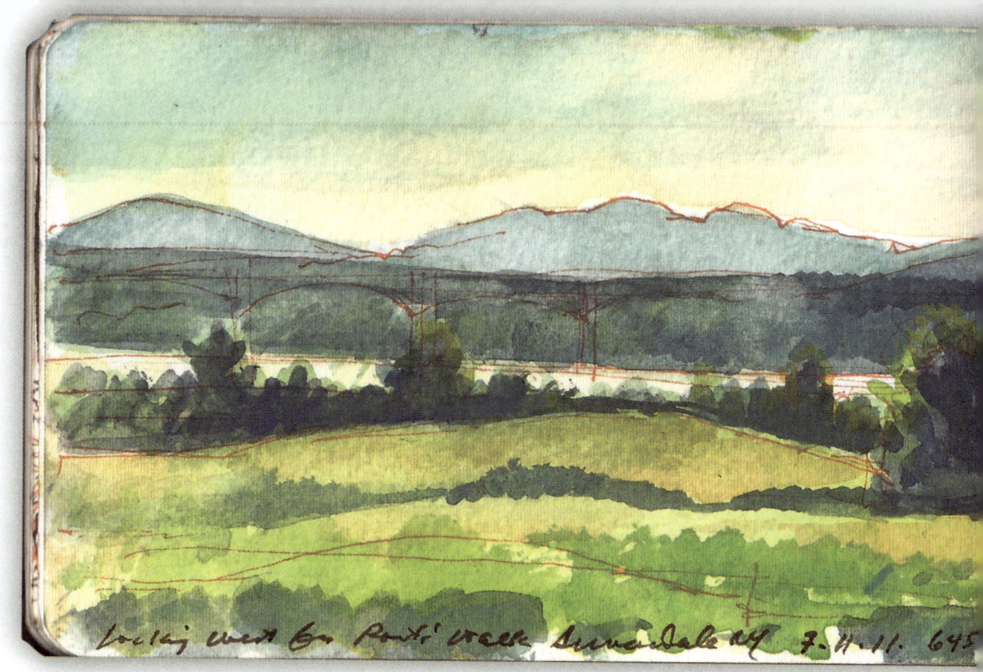

Fig. 16.

POETS' WALK

Located on the left bank of the Hudson a few miles above the Kingston-Rhinecliff Bridge is a rolling tract of land that was first developed into a private pleasure park in 1849. Wealthy families having built estates atop the bluffs decided to set aside a tract of uncultivated land for the enjoyment of nature and the improvement of health. German landscape architect Hans Jacob Ehler divided the land between clearings and woodlands, laying out trails, view sheds, and pavilions. Washington Irving, William Cullen Bryant, and other notable recipients of Delano and Astor hospitality are said to have drawn inspiration from rambles at Poets' Walk. In recent years the park has come under the control of Scenic Hudson Land Trust, which maintains the

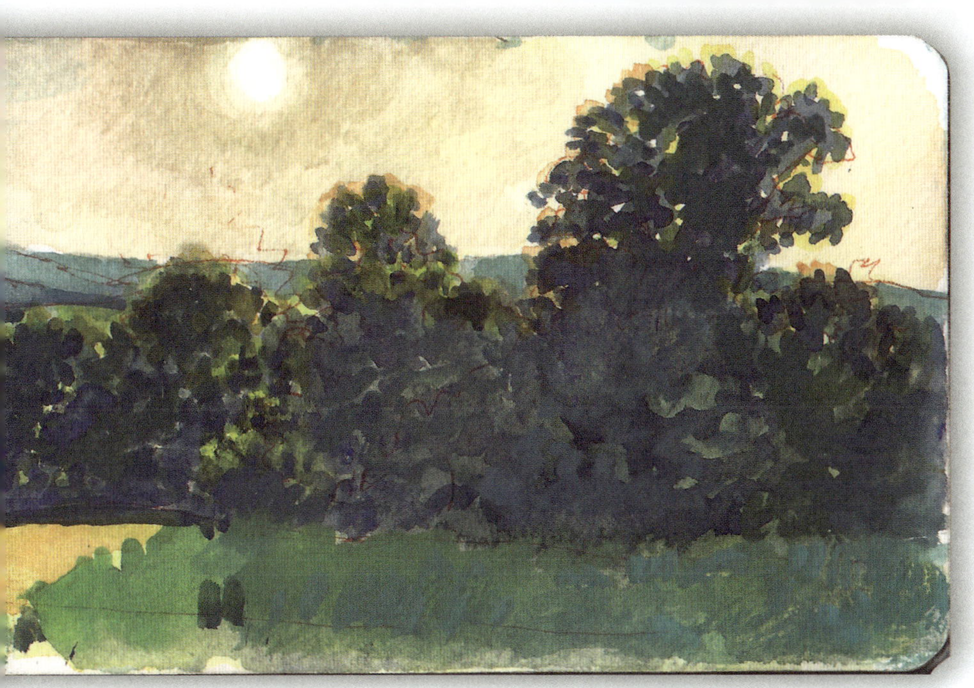

trails and other amenities for year-round public use. Having visited the park on numerous occasions, I have never failed to meet other hikers on the trails without the exchange of pleasant greetings. Working from one of the wooden benches set out along the trails, or on the portable stool strapped to my back, I was never interrupted or distracted by other visitors. They might slow their pace to steal a glance as they pass by, with a nod or a smile. Such places seem to promote civility as much as they inspire bards.

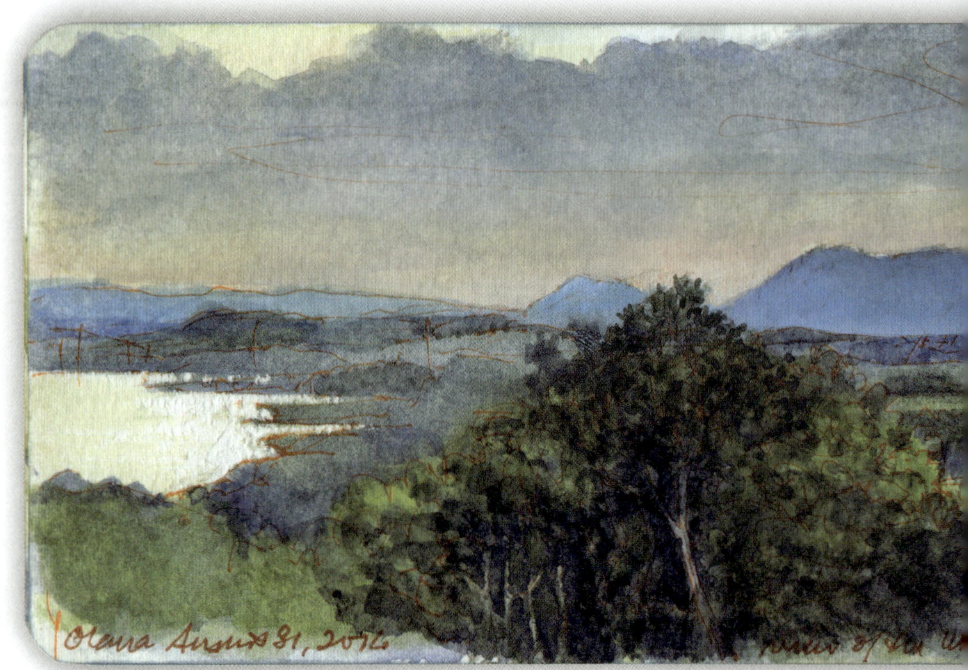

Fig. 17.

CATSKILL ESCARPMENT FROM OLANA

> Nature has been very lavish here in the gift of her beauty—I am sure you would enjoy the noble scenes which our windows command.
> —Frederic Edwin Church to Henry Wadsworth Longfellow, 1880

Sitting on the edge of the south porch at Olana—the home of Hudson River school painter Frederic Edwin Church, the warm day seems to threaten rain. The day is warm, threatening rain. Wednesday. We had just driven up from the city to deliver Kathie to a meeting. The previous week we had been in London, Kew, and Greenwich. Like the Royal Observatory, Olana crowns a hill that spills steeply down a wide, grassy slope. The difference here is that

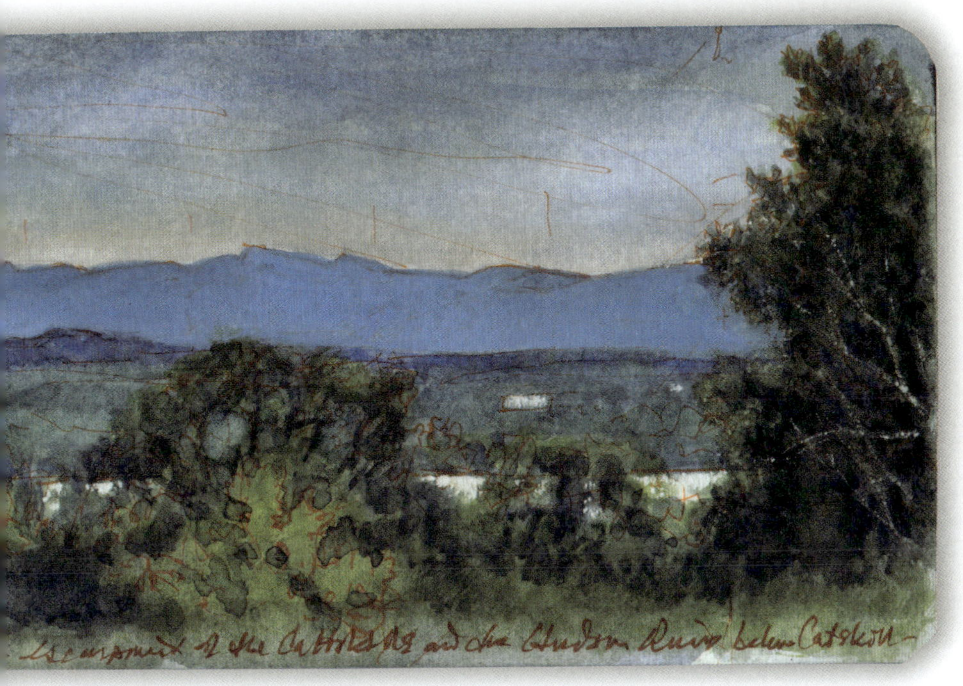

I am not looking across the river at the Isle of Dogs, with the new Docklands rising up behind it to the north. Dark clouds to the west seem to promise approaching thunder and rain. Visitors on a guided tour of the house peer over my shoulder. No one pauses to give me advice, or ask me what I'm doing. Just part of the scenery. A young couple walks to the edge of the hilltop. They take a selfie. A drop of rain lands on the back of my hand.

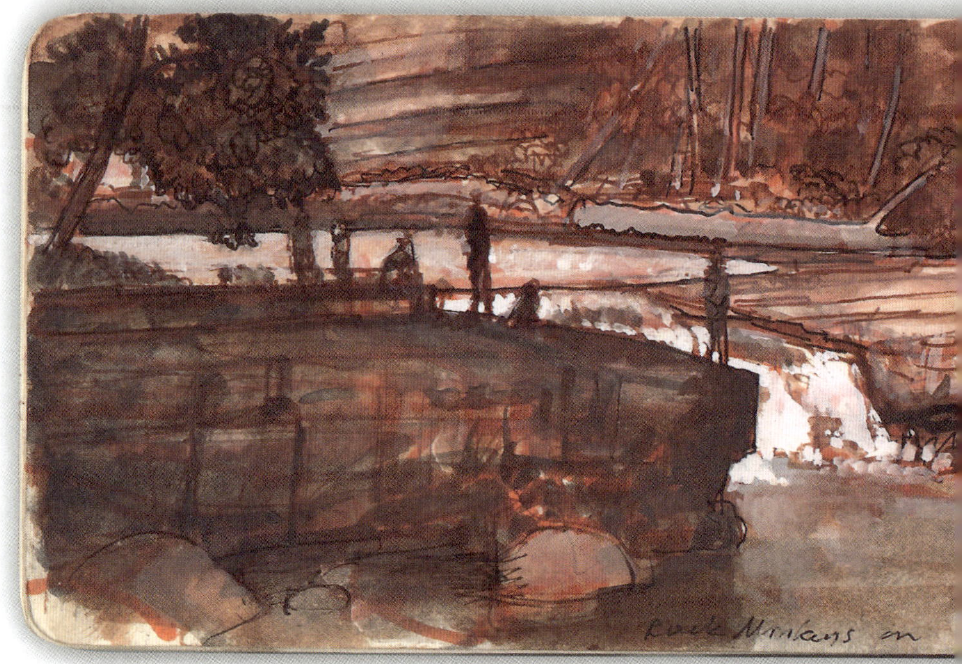

Fig. 18.

RONDOUT CREEK BELOW HIGH FALLS

Rondout Creek is born at the confluence of Sandburg Creek and Shingle Gully, just east of Ellenville. The stream flows in a northerly direction through Kerhonkson and Accord, north of which it turns abruptly to the east, falling in a vertical drop of 20 feet into a swift declivity hewn through sedimentary limestone. Inclined stratifications bend and buckle as trees cling to its walls. Every summer bathers gather on the rocky ledges bordering the creek, defiant of its dangers and of local ordinances. A hundred yards downstream from this place two stone bridgeheads stand opposite one another across the creek—once linked by a canal bridge carrying barge traffic between Honesdale, Pennsylvania, and Kingston, New York. Almost like a

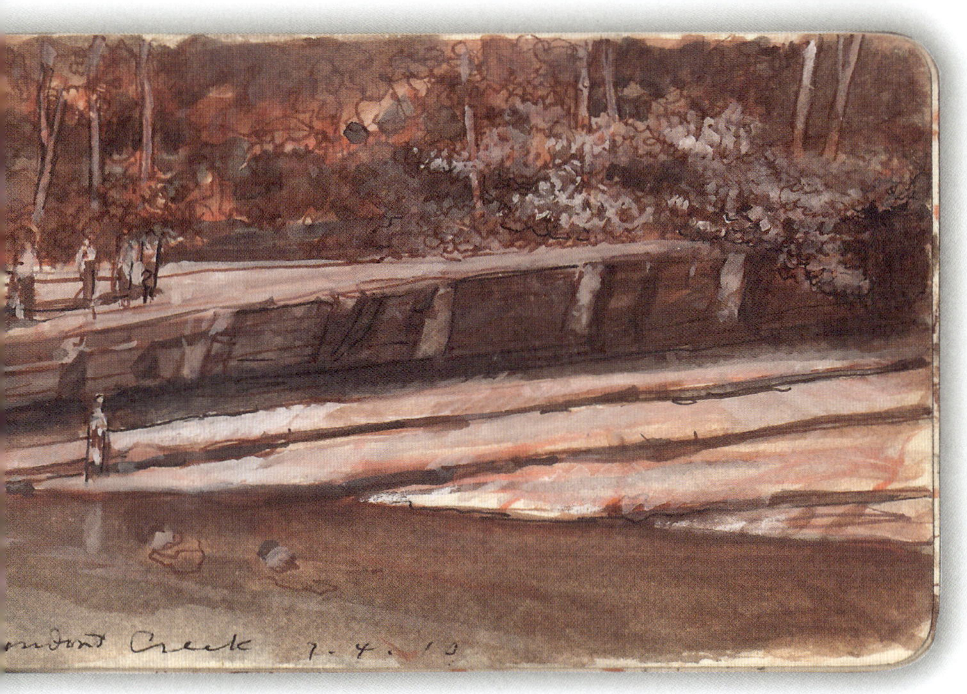

pagan rite of passage, young divers would run along the towpath, leaping from the tower to plunge into the stream. Every year it seemed that someone either lost their life, or suffered crippling injury by misjudging their trajectory and colliding with submerged rocks. On a visit to High Falls, the eponymous village where modernist artist Marc Chagall sometimes summered, I noticed a hurricane fence, built to enclose the erstwhile diving platform.

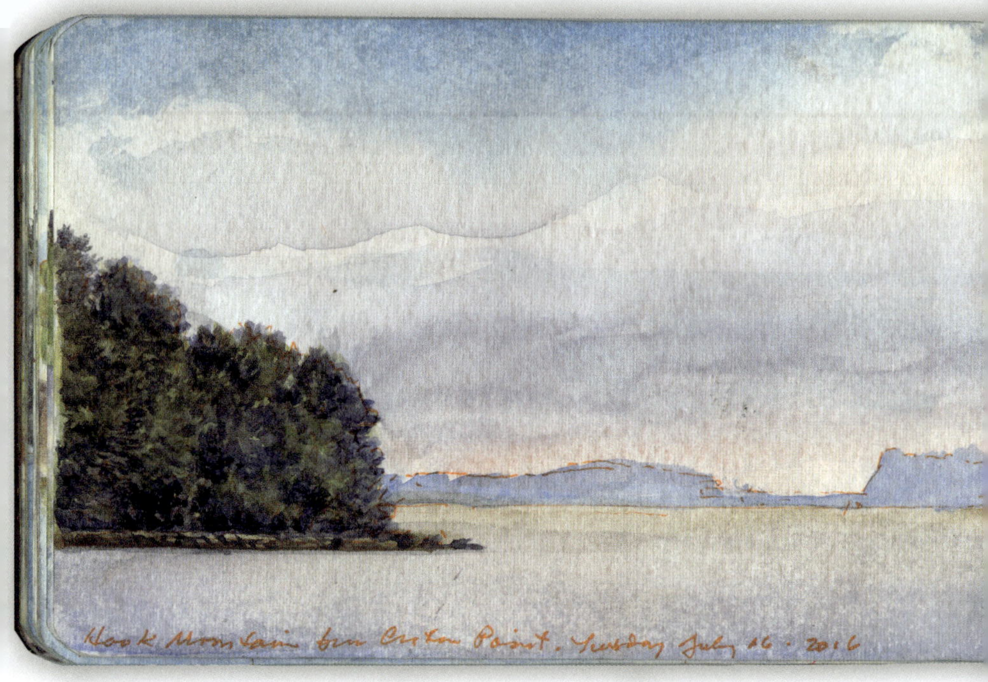

Fig. 19.

HOOK MOUNTAIN FROM CROTON POINT

Extending from Nyack to the Tors towering over West Haverstraw, Hook Mountain is considered part of the Palisades that end just south of Piermont. A sheer basaltic escarpment, crowned by a narrow ridge, its name was inspired by its appearance on maps—as an inverted hook, with its point at High Tor.

Located just north of the mouth of Croton River, the hilly peninsula known as Croton Point reaches out from the left bank, in a southwesterly direction. Marking the division between Tappan Zee and Haverstraw Bay, the land today is maintained by Westchester as a county park. The name is an Anglicization of Kenotin—the name of an indigenous tribal leader who lived

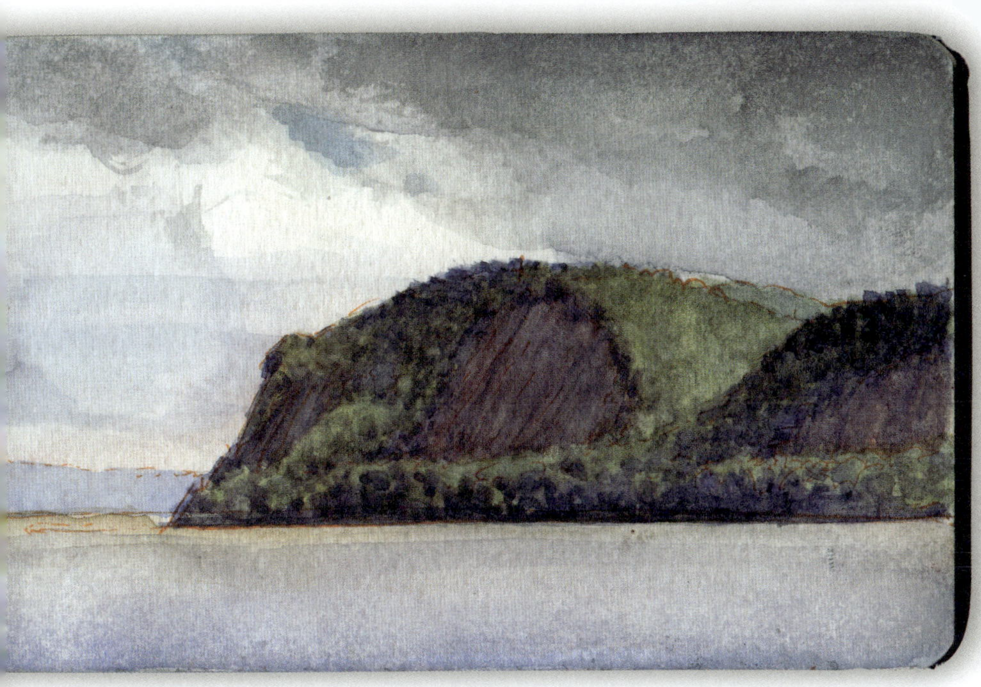

near the mouth of the eponymous river during colonial days. The cluster of trees seen to the left is Crawbuckie Park. Far in the distance, across the Tappan Zee, is Tallman Mountain, the northern end of the Palisades. Traveling upriver, the lower Hudson is a series of seas and bays, from Raritan Bay through The Narrows, from the harbor into North River channel. Beyond lies Tappan Zee, Haverstraw Bay, and Peekskill Bay. To be precise, here the Hudson is not a river, but a tidal estuary reaching another 130 miles upstream.

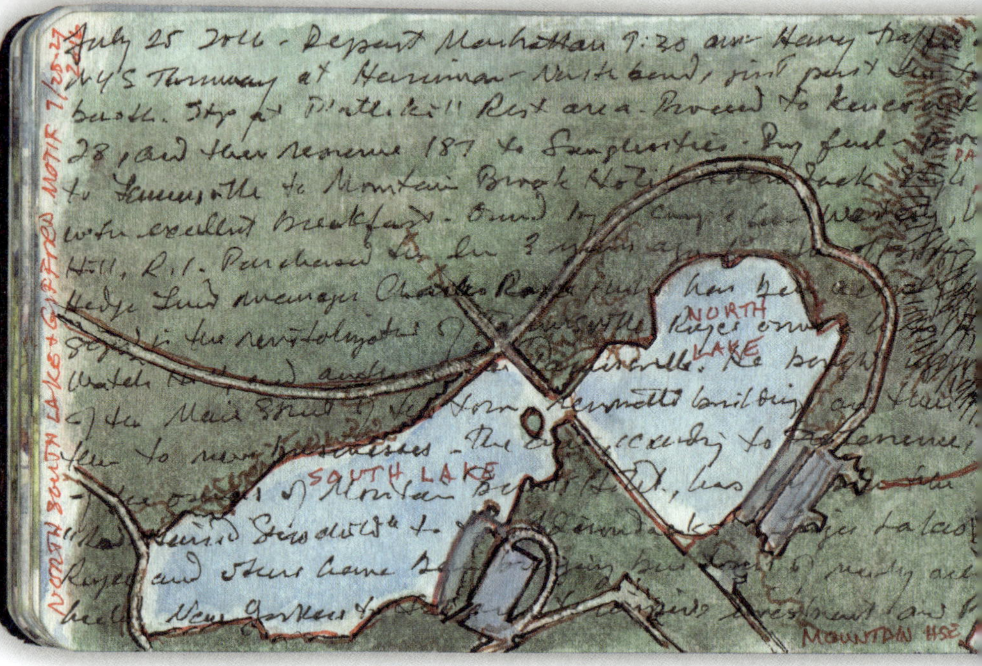

Fig. 20.

PICTORIAL MAP OF NORTH-SOUTH LAKE

Extending westward from the Catskill Escarpment, twin lakes rest in a broad vale between North and South Mountains. On its eastern rim, the Catskill Mountain House site is now a wide grassy ledge. Westward, the land rises toward Tannersville. Before European invaders built settlements in the mountains, indigenous people farmed the bottomlands and hunted game in the heights. Dutch expansion into the region sparked native resistance, which quickly escalated into bloody warfare. Crops were destroyed. Settlements scattered, clearing the way for modern economies. Exploring the mountains in search of new plant species, Philadelphia naturalist John Bartram had visited the Catskills in 1753, visiting North-South Lake. Fourteen-year-old

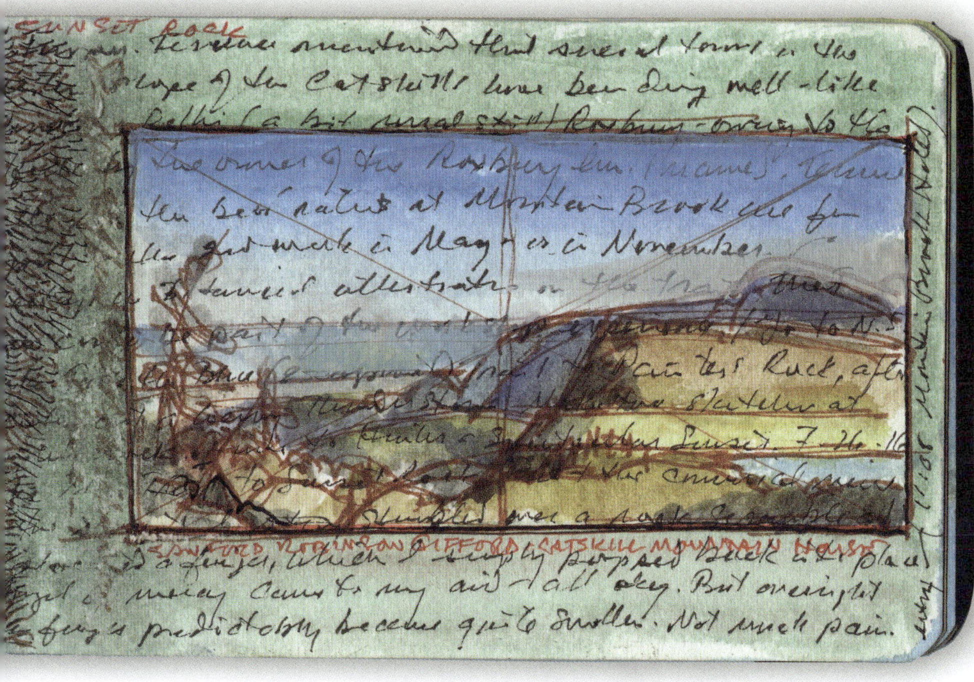

Billy had demonstrated a passion for drawing. Attracted to a large tree fungus known botanically as *Auricularia auricula-judae*, the boy was about to test it with his foot when his father pulled him back, away from a coiled rattlesnake. Despite pleas for mercy from both father and son, their rustic guide slew the creature. Making notes on the site during a visit in 2016, I decided to add a map in overlay; beside it a thumbnail of Sanford Gifford's view from Sunset Rock.

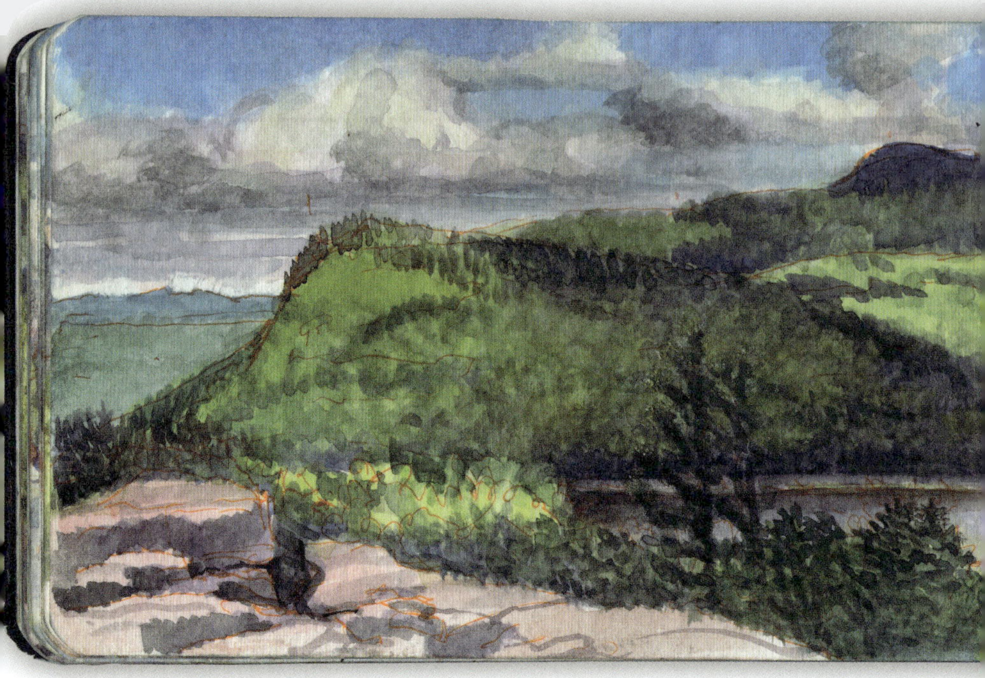

Fig. 21.

NORTH-SOUTH LAKE FROM SUNSET ROCK

On the southeast shoulder of North Mountain is an outcropping of exposed rocks, approached by a trail that follows the rim of the Catskill escarpment running north from the former site of the grand Catskill Mountain House, built in 1824 and burned to ashes in 1963. Halfway along the trail is a rocky ledge known as Painters Rock, with a sheer drop of 200 feet. From here the trail rises, over rock-fall and ledges. Climbing higher, the trail loops around a wall of sedimentary limestone, the floor of a vanished sea. Ascending to the rim of this formation, the trail enters a wooded understory of carpeted ferns and other leafy plants. Crisscrossing trails backtrack to an open, deeply-fissured rocky platform. At its edge rests Susnset Rock, an object that was painted by Thomas

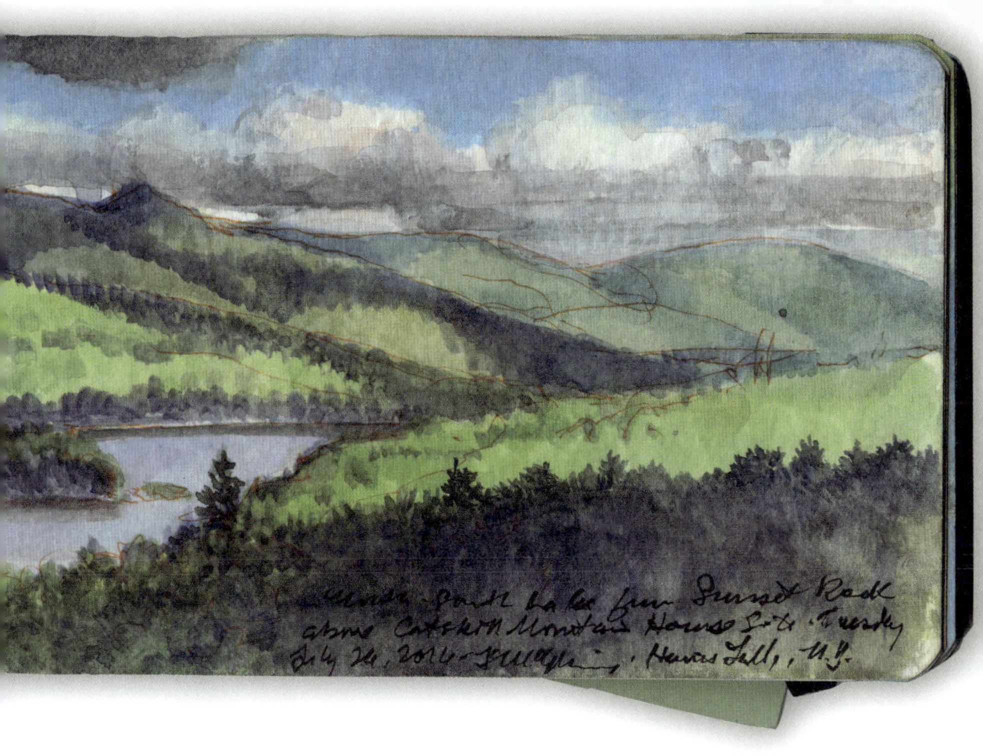

Cole, Sanford Gifford, and other Hudson River School painters. One would never know it was the same boulder. Descending the trail, I lost my footing on a rock scramble and dislocated a finger. Popping the digit back into place, I continued down the mountain. Later along the shore of North Lake, a couple recounted having spent a night on the mountain with their injured dog, sans food, water, or shelter, menaced by bears. With nothing worse than a sore and swollen finger, I felt lucky.

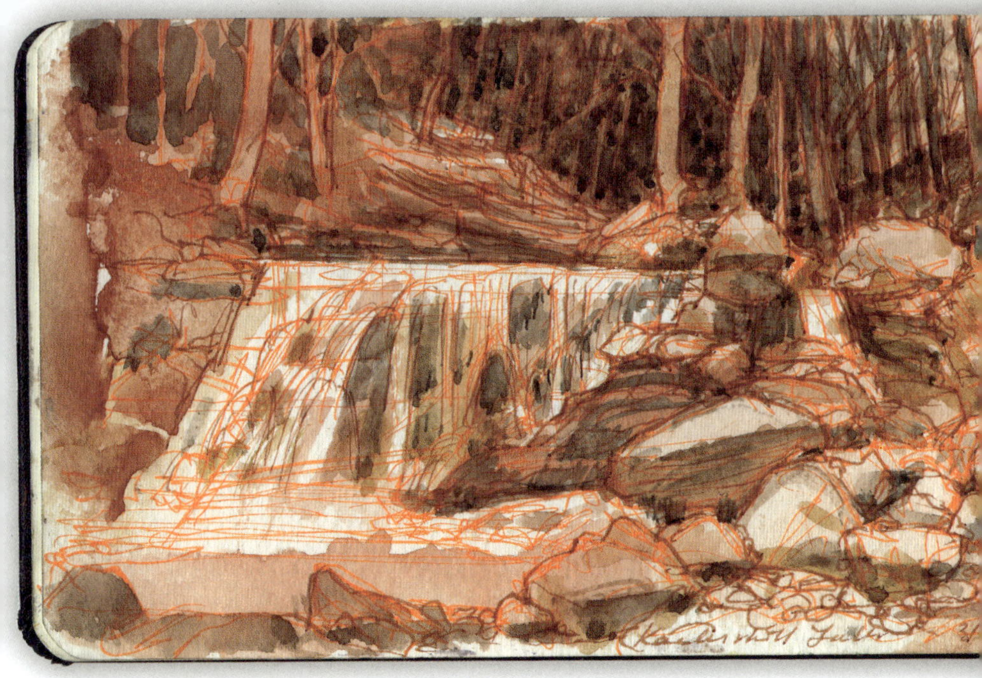

Fig. 22.

LOWER CATARACT, KAATERSKILL CREEK

North-South Lake drains into Spruce Creek, which flows southward for roughly a mile, before plunging over a rocky precipice into a shallow pool on a broad ledge of rock, over which it cascades into a rocky defile known as Kaaterskill Clove. The combined height of the falls is 260 feet, nearly 80 feet taller than Niagara. Below the second falls the creek assumes a new identity, sharing its name with the gorge it has carved out of the eastern escarpment of the Catskill mountains. Descending the gorge via a series of smaller falls and cataracts, treacherous waters give way to a chain of swimming holes before the stream meanders across the floodplain and into the Hudson, at the village of Catskill.

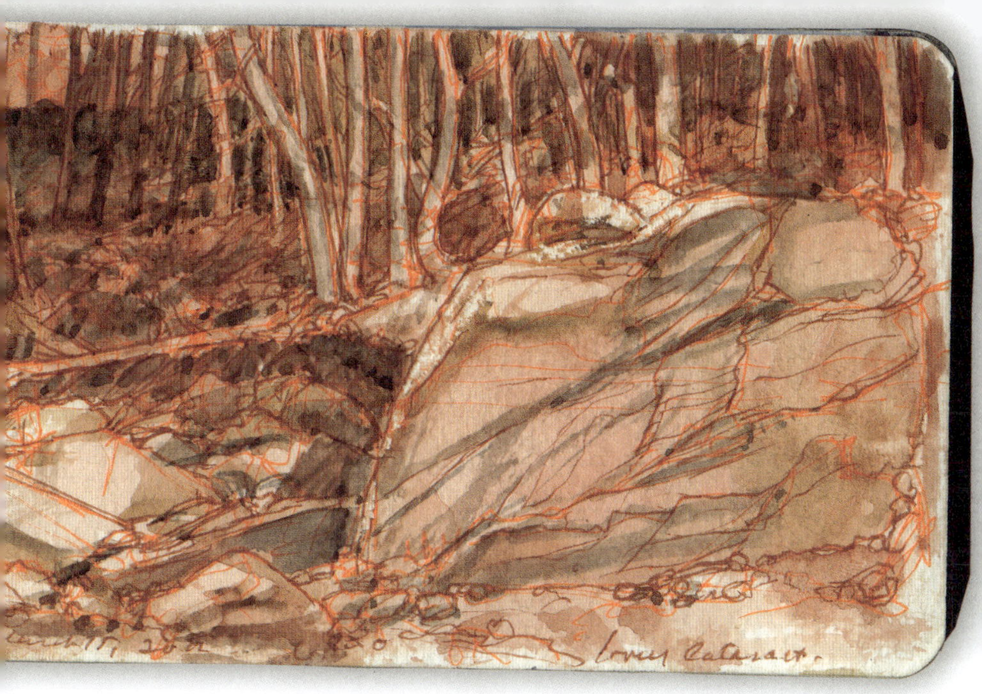

British-born Thomas Cole (1801–1848) had moved from England to Ohio with his family, but soon made his way east, to study in Philadelphia before settling in New York. The year after William Guy Wall published the last set of six prints in his Hudson River Portfolio—the same year the Erie Canal opened to traffic—Cole ventured upriver to visit what were well on their way to becoming bucket-list destinations. Both Sunset Rock and Kaaterskill Falls were within an easy walk of the Catskill Mountain House hotel. While he was not the first artist to behold these wonders, he was the first to establish them within the canon of American landscape painting.

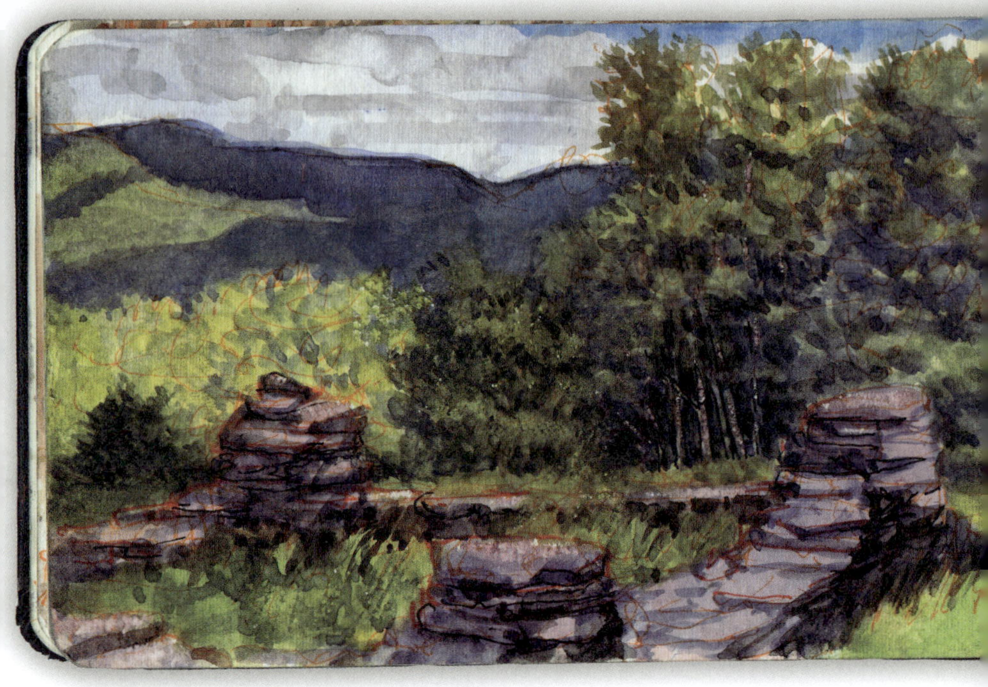

Fig. 23.

JOHN BURROUGHS GRAVESITE

Parking along the shoulder of Burroughs Memorial Road just west of Roxbury, New York, Kathie and I follow a track through the woods to a wide cleaing. Hewn by the east branch of the Delaware River and the headwaters of Schoharie Creek, the little valley below us feeds two might watersheds—the Delaware and the Hudson.

Born on a farm nearby, literary naturalist John Burroughs (1837–1921) was inspired by Catskill ramble and Hudson Valley sojourns, to remind countless readers how close observation draws us nearer to nature, in ways that develop the mind and nourish the soul.

When a neighbor complained that birds no longer visited her home, Burroughs

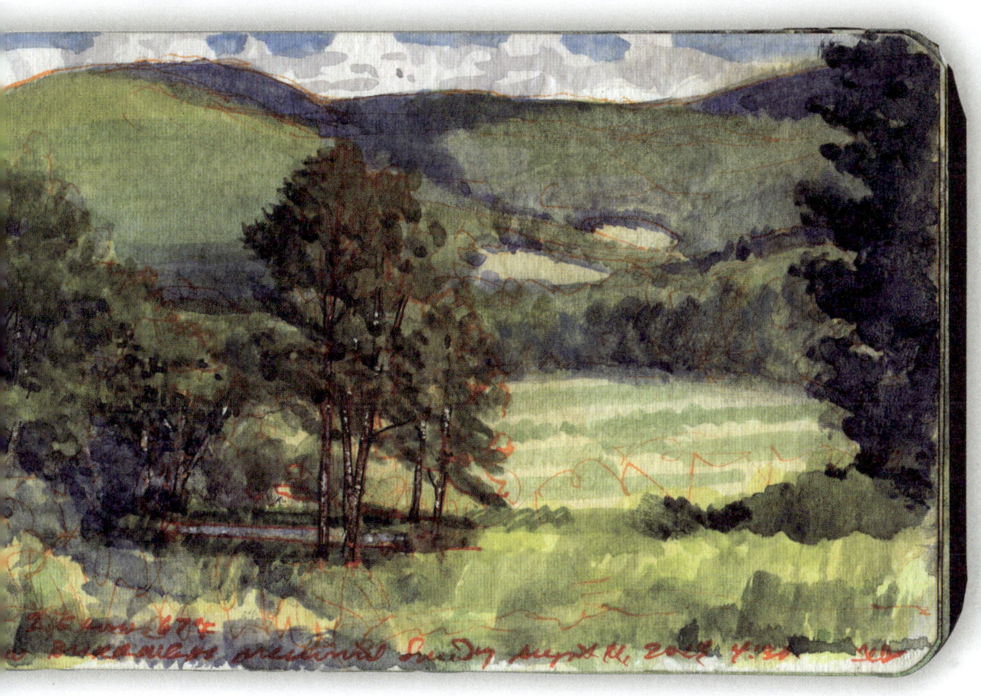

replied that during their conversation he had noted the songs of several and named the species one by one. "You must have the bird in your heart," he told her, "before you can find it in the bush." Toward the end of his life Burroughs retired to Woodchuck Lodge, a rustic farmhouse on the slopes of Clump Mountain, near the place of his birth. His fondest retreat was a large recumbent boulder dubbed Boyhood Rock. Resting beside it now for nearly a century, his mortal dust returns to the earth. Burroughs is gone. Yet something lingers, to welcome new friends, alert to nature's wonders.

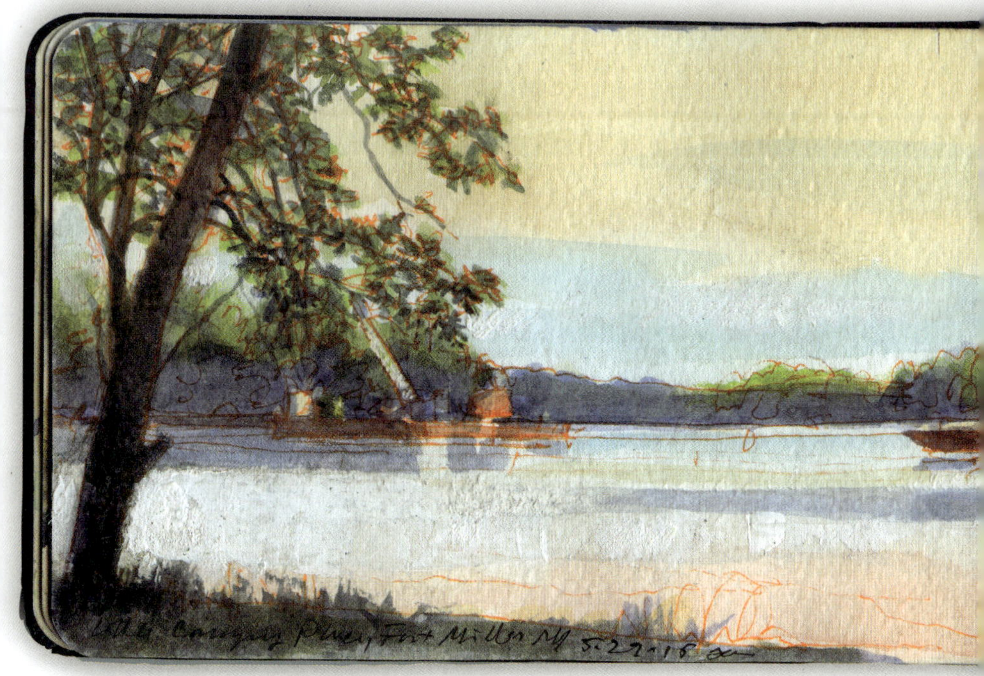

Fig. 24.

THE HUDSON NEAR FORT MILLER

Preparing to produce a series of prints with accompanying texts, Irish painter William Guy Wall journeyed with travel writer John Agg from New York City to the Adirondacks in 1820. Fort Miller had been constructed along the Hudson during the French and Indian War to protect a river crossing, or carrying place above a small set of falls. The region was famous in the prelude to Burgoyne's surrender at Schuylerville, four days and two years before Cornwallis laid down his arms at Yorktown. Burgoyne's failure brought France into an alliance with the newly formed United States. The area between the Mohawk River and Lake Champlain would soon become more well known through the Leatherstocking novels of James Fenimore Cooper. Now, as then, Fort Miller

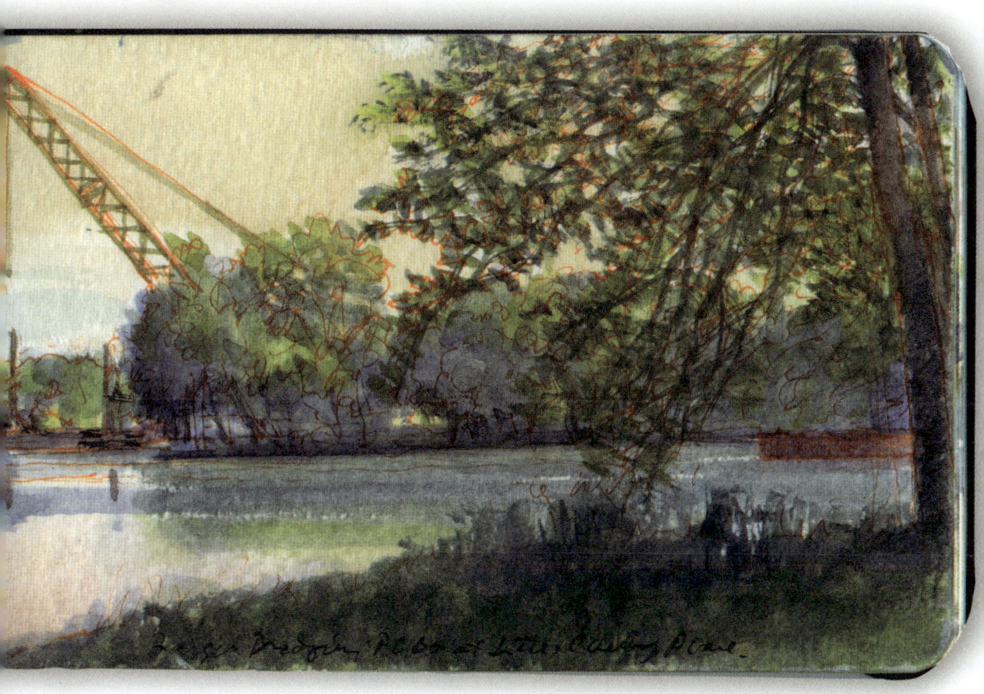

is a pleasant hamlet on the banks of the Hudson, next to one of the locks on the Champlain Canal that links tidewater Hudson to Lake Champlain. Architectural historian, novelist, and raconteur James Howard Kunstler has for many years been a plein air painting companion. On May 27, 2015, we piled into his pickup truck and headed off in search of a motif. Arriving at Clark's Mills, discouraged by new fences and threatening signage, we moved upriver to Fort Miller. A pair of dredging barges ride on the stream, cranes at rest, cables slack, these dystopic gatecrashers, disrupting pastoral harmony with rusting dissonance remind us that the Hudson is a going concern, a working waterway that mingles beauty with muscle.

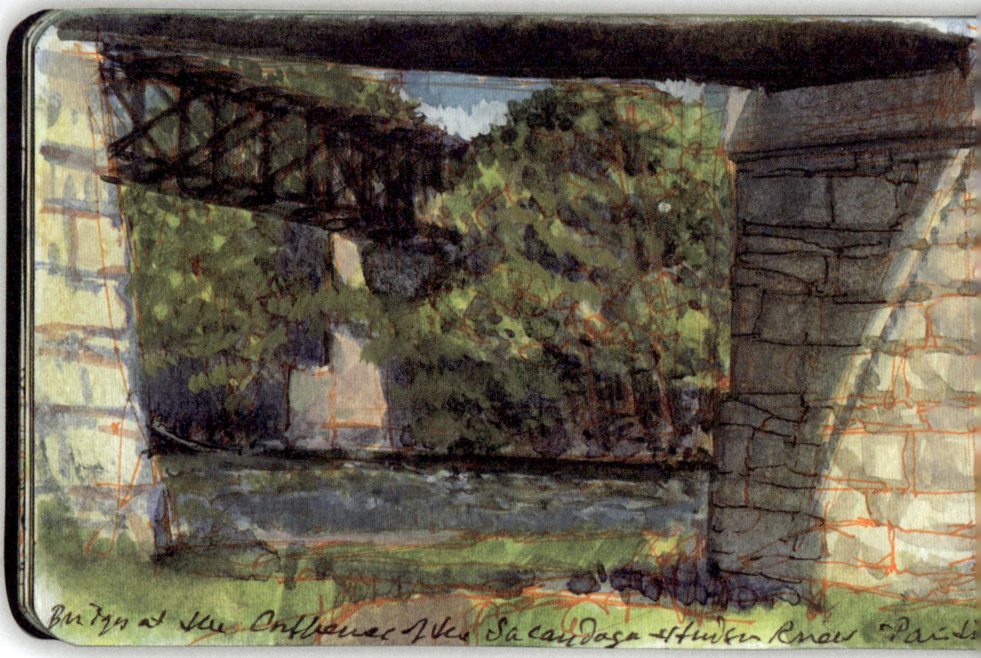

Fig. 25.

TWIN BRIDGES NEAR THE MOUTH OF THE

Traveling down the Hudson in 1820 with Irish landscape painter William Guy Wall, travel writer John Agg describes the land around the mouth of the Sacandaga as

> broken and precipitous; and the natural course of the current is impeded and distracted by large fragments of stone, which choke up the narrow channel. The character of the scenery is wild, ferocious, and solitary sublimity; lofty and irregular acclivities, covered the gloomy verdure of interminable forests and glens; over whose terrific depths unchanging darkness lowers.

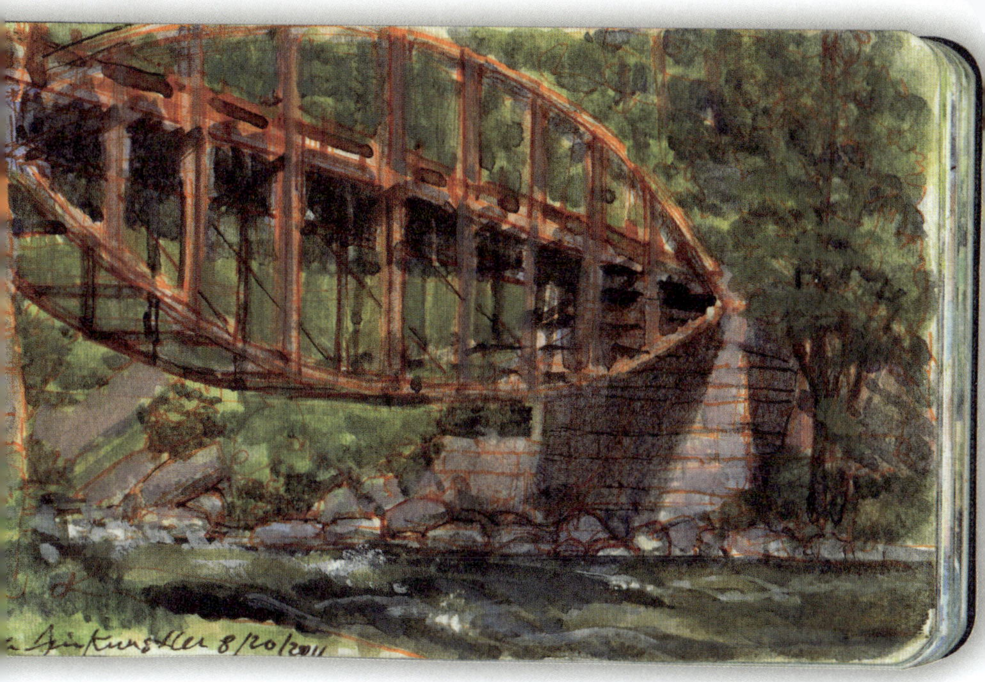

SACANDAGA RIVER

Visiting the site with author and painter James Howard Kunstler, we found two bridges crossing the Sacandaga. A parabolic lenticular bow-truss bridge, built in 1885, had replaced the covered bridge seen by Agg and Wall in 1820. Falling into disrepair, the bridge was closed to traffic in 1994. Five years later, Saratoga County considered replacing the bridge, until preservationists raised funds for its restoration. The bridge reopened to traffic in 2005. Beyond is a deck truss steel bridge, built in 1943. Both spans rest on masonry stone piers. Parking along the shoulder of the Old Corinth Road, we descended a steep embankment and set up on a grassy rise just east of the bridgehead. A few hundred years from the village of Hadley, the setting retained a sense of wildness, save for the Anthropocene geometry of these twin bridges.

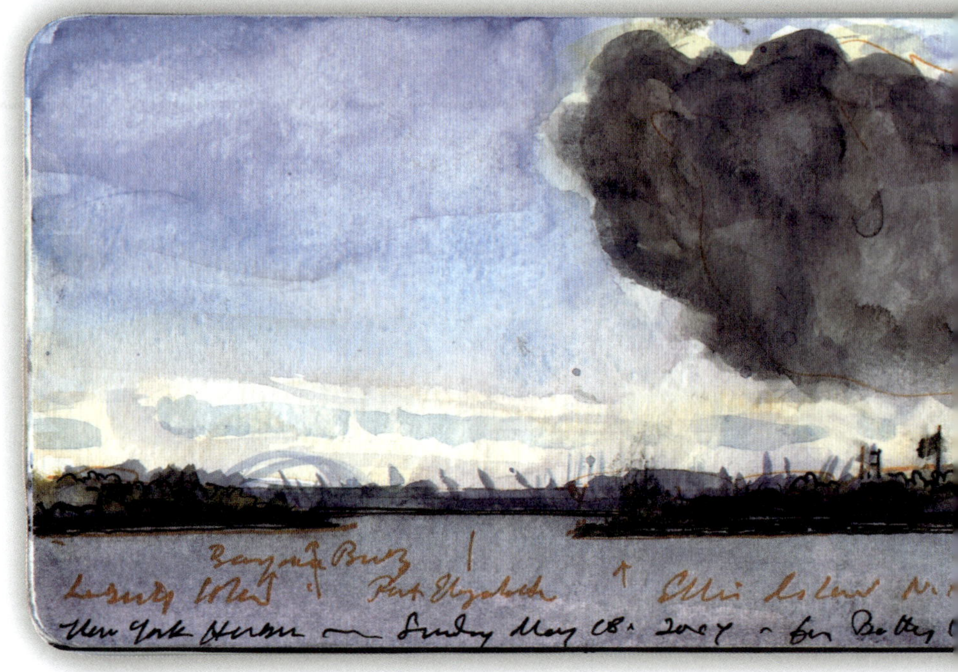

Fig. 26.

NEW YORK HARBOR: ELLIS ISLAND

Oyster Island, also known as Ellis Island, was first fortified in 1795, in preparation for what came to be known as the Quasi-War with France. Acquired by the federal government in 1808, a twenty-gun battery was established, which in concert with the guns of Castle Williams on Governor's Island and Castle Clinton at the Battery in lower Manhattan, created a killzone at the mouth of the Hudson River. While it saw no action during the War of 1812, the island served as a prisoner-of-war camp during the conflict. In 1861 Fort Gibson was decommissioned and repurposed as a naval weapons depot. A flood of immigration into New York City had by 1890 far exceeded the capacity of Castle Garden. A new immigration inspection

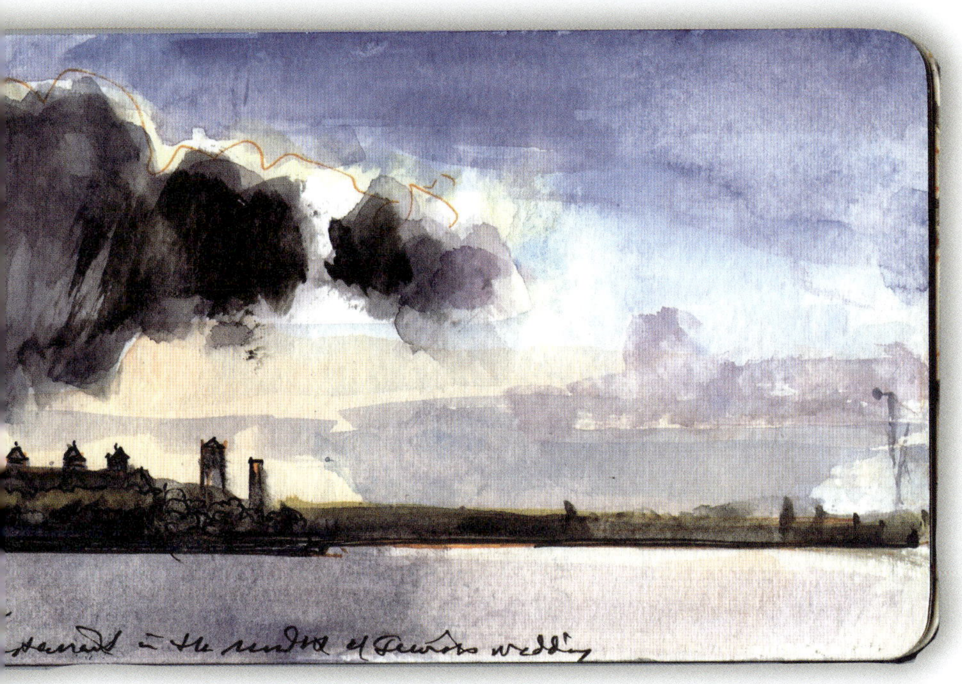

station opened its doors in 1892. Ellis Island remained in service until 1954.

More than twelve million arrivals passed through its gates to become permanent residents and citizens of the United States. Today the site is part of Statue of Liberty National Monument, and is accessible only by water.

This painting was made in Battery Park, looking across New York harbor, from beside the East Coast Memorial, honoring members of the US Merchant Marine and Army Transport Service who perished in coastal waters during the Second World War.

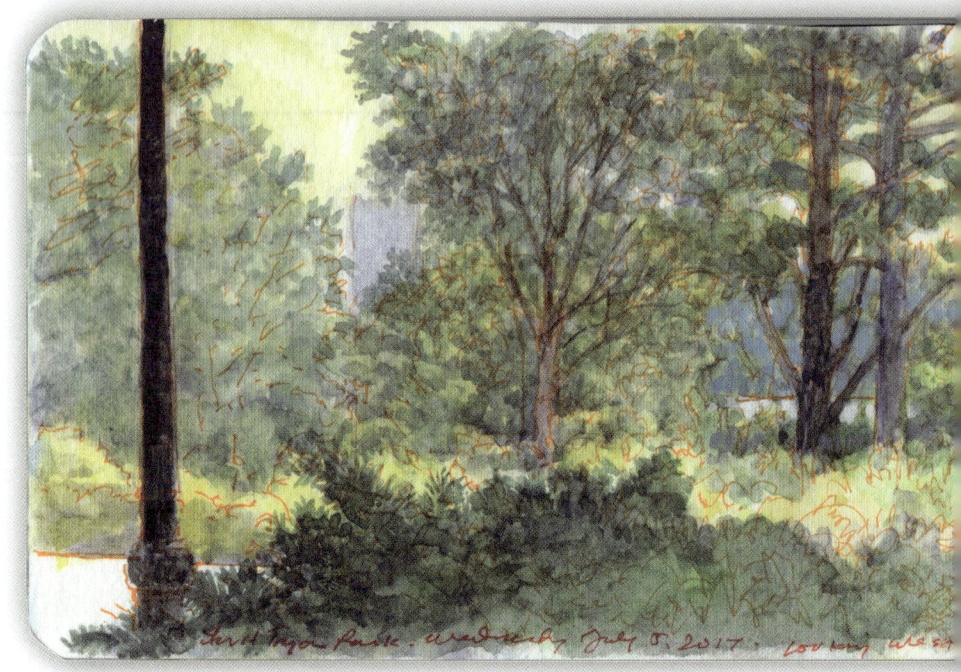

Fig. 27.

THE HEATHER GARDEN: FORT TRYON PARK

Northern Manhattan possesses nearly 500 acres of parklands, divided primarily between Highbridge Park, Fort Tryon Park, and Inwood Hill Park, together with smaller parks and green spaces scattered across the island above 155th Street. Since the 1970s, nonprofit conservancies have played a key role in locating nongovernment funding for the maintenance and improvement of New York parklands. The New York Restoration Project planted a million trees, making New York one of the greenest cities in the nation. The Heather Garden and Alpine Garden in Fort Tryon Park attract thousands of visitors every year.

While I worked on this painting one hot summer day, my wife sat beside

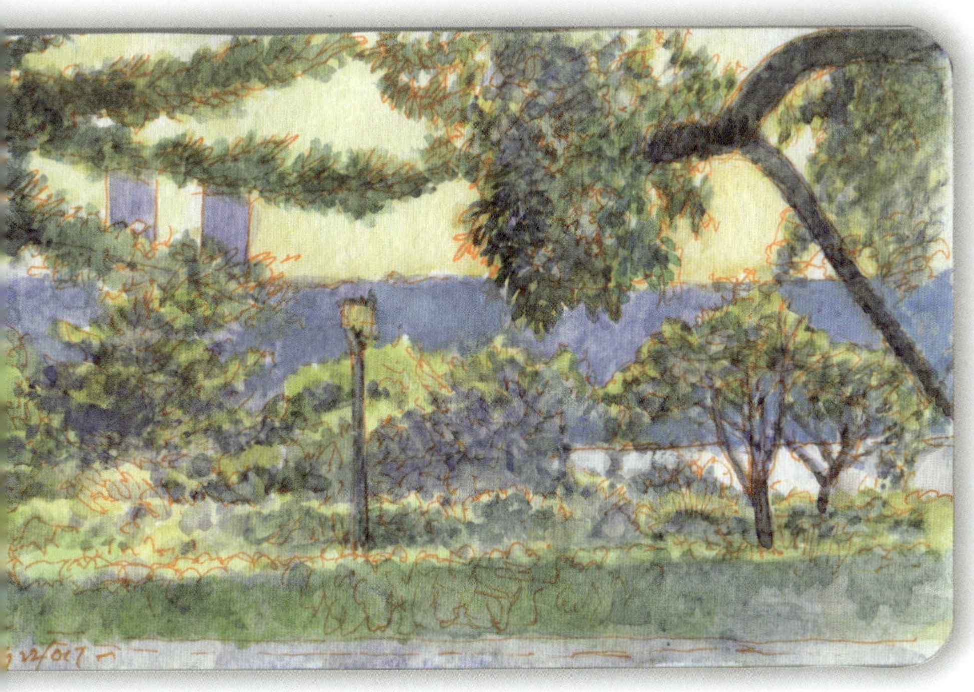

me, reading a book. Crying out suddenly, she pointed to a small snake writhing on the hot asphalt, being cooked to death under a burning sun. I rushed over, lifted it carefully with the end of my brush, and laid it under a bush. Sprinkling the creature with cool water, I studied its form, the shape of its tiny head, narrow neck, taupe coloring, the paired markings running down either side of its spine. What are you? I wondered. And suddenly, I knew. It was a timber rattlesnake. These creatures are not hatched from eggs but born live, a dozen at a time. I wondered. Where's your mother? Where's the rest of your family? Revived, the little serpent flicked its tongue and disappeared into a stone wall. The Bartrams would have approved.

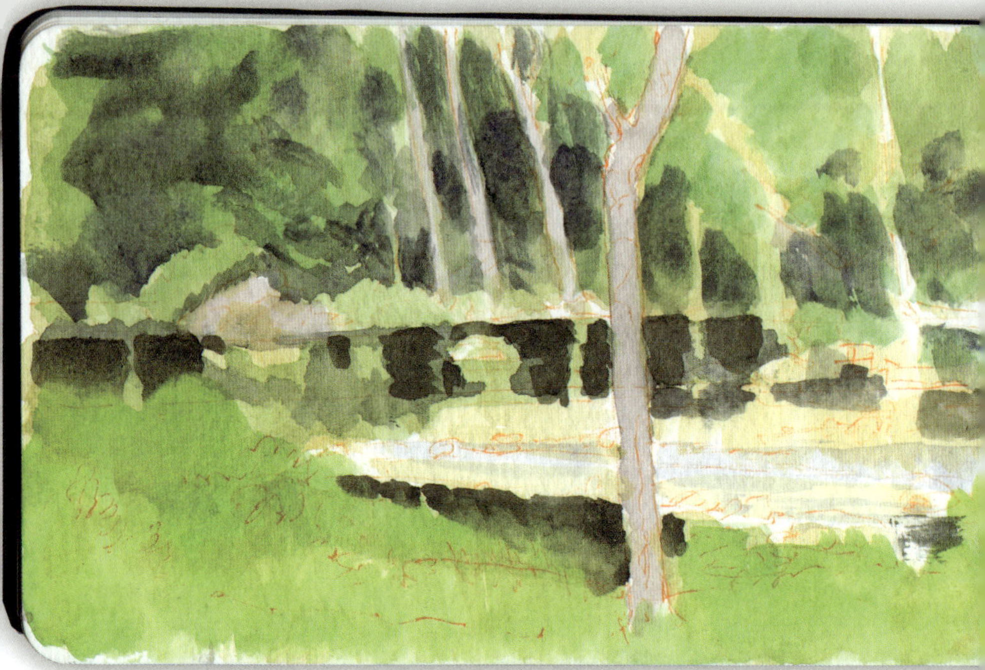

Fig. 28.

THE WEST FORK OF THE HUDSON RIVER:

The source of the Hudson was firmly established until 1872, when watershed conservationist Verplanck Colvin identified Lake Tear of the Clouds as its "well-spring." The Hudson River is formed by the confluence of a number of streams, the largest of which issues from Henderson Lake, northeast of Newcomb village, and Catlin Lake to the northwest.

In 1859 travel writer and artist Benson J. Lossing journeyed from New York City to the heart of the Adirondacks, and back again. His young wife was said to be the second nonindigenous woman known to have reached the summit of Mount Marcy. At Newcomb, the Bensons engaged famed Native American guide Mitchell Sabattis, who later trekked the mountains with

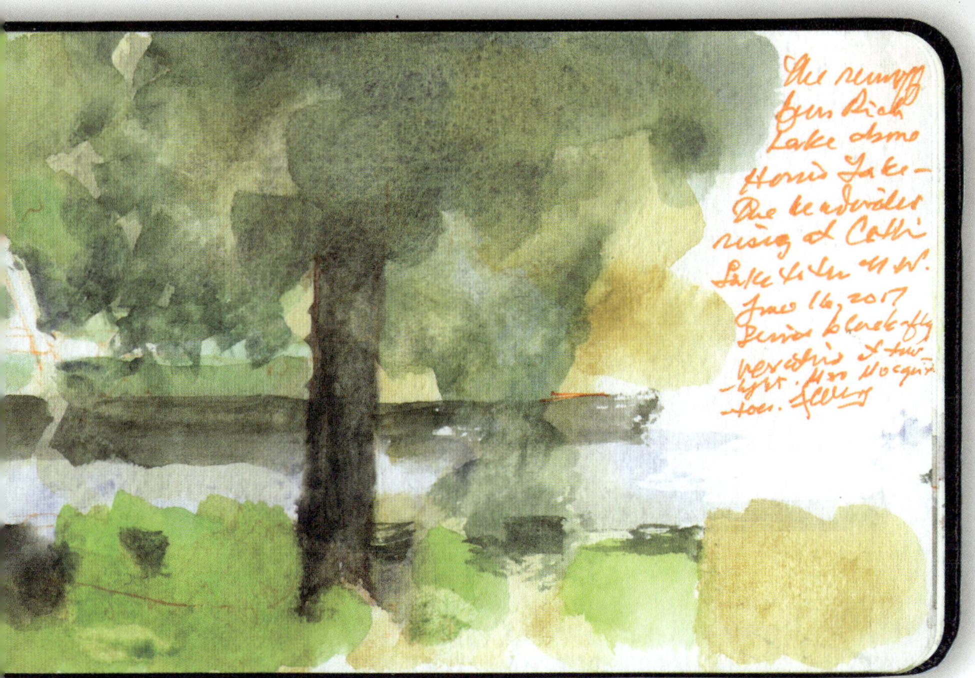

NEWCOMB, NEW YORK

Winslow Homer. This painted sketch was made near Newcomb, along a channel flowing into Harris Lake from Rich Lake, site of the Adirondack Interpretive Center, operated by the State University of New York College of Environmental Science and Forestry. The center runs an artist residency program, exhibitions, lectures, and other events. As I worked on this sketch, a young man paddled up to the bank in front of my rested cabin. Dragging his canoe onshore, cursing the blackflies in a barrage of blue language, he ran off, disappearing into the woods.

Chapter 5

WORK PAGES

Go outdoors. Take a line for a walk. Make this part of your daily practice. Write what you behold. Draw what you hear, whatever comes to mind. Think of your personal field-book as a hand-held device powered only mindfulness, alert to your surroundings. Take a chance. Make a mark. To make a bad drawing is impossible because there are only great drawings and research. The same holds true for writing. Taking note of our surroundings, drawing and writing sets us off in new directions, to meet ourselves along the trail. When the path leads us to beauty, we find wonders. Where we can share these with others, we find art. Take a trust-fall. Get busy. As John Burroughs said "Leap, and the net will appear."

Never lose the first impression which has moved you.

—J. B. C. Corot

A hill or tree cannot make a good painting just because it is a hill or tree. It is lines and colors put together so that they may say something.

—Georgia O'Keeffe

*To learn something new,
take the path that you
took yesterday.*

—John Burroughs

Sketch everything and keep your curiosity fresh.

—John Singer Sargent

...I haven't seen an object until I actually start painting it.

—Janet Fish

...we look at a given landscape
and take possession of it in
our blood and brain.

—M. Scott Momaday

One looks, looks long, and the world comes in.

—Joseph Campbell

It's not what you look at that matters, it's what you see.

—Henry David Thoreau

All journeys have secret destinations of which the traveler is unaware.

—Martin Buber

All art is but dirtying the paper delicately.

—John Ruskin

Chapter 6

MATERIALS & EQUIPMENT

The mission of the sketchbook traveler is to devote as much time to engaging with their surroundings, not struggling with bulky box easels, umbrellas, and any gear other than a small messenger bag, or multi-pocket travel vest. Here are the essentials:

- Sketchbook
- Drawing tools
- Pocket paintbox
- Travel brushes
- Water bottle for painting
- Bottle for drinking water
- Accessories: sponge, safety razor, beeswax stick, clips, folding pocketknife, compass, maps, camera and/or mobile phone, field glasses, etc.
- Multipocket travel vest (doubles as a rucksack)
- Messenger bag or small knapsack (for additional burdens)
- Insect repellent and sunscreen
- Folding tripod stool

DRESS FOR THE FIELD

Wear comfortable, practical clothing. Nineteenth-century artist-explorers wore the equivalent of hunting attire—a pullover frock coat, wide-brimmed round hat for protection from the sun, a shirt and cravat that could double as a windbreaker scarf, stout boots or high-quarter shoes worn with gathers to cover the ankle. In period engravings, we can see artists wearing backpacks, onto which was strapped a collapsible umbrella that could be mounted onto their walking sticks, along with a folding tripod stool.

- Contemporary options are a lighter and more portable. This book is addressed to anyone who wants to deepen and enrich their experience of travel through drawing and writing, not only to urban sketchers and plein air painters, for which there exists a universe of paraphernalia. The following is focused specifically on outdoor garments and accessories for traveling light, on a sketchbook safari, carrying everything you might need on your person. Travelers visiting more settled areas like towns and cities can wear whatever street clothes suits their fancy, perhaps with the addition of a small shoulder bag or travel vest. Favor function over fashion, with the caveat that practical clothing has a style all its own. Please consult the list of suppliers in the back of this book.

- UV-PROOF AND INSECT-RESISTANT GARMENTS: Well-constructed long-sleeve cargo shirts and cargo trousers are recommended. A number of companies make clothing for fishermen that are also permeated with insect repellent. In places where temperatures fluctuate greatly, and/or rapid changes in weather are common, be sure to dress in layers.

- TRAVEL VEST: A wide array is available from a variety of suppliers. Look for strong construction and lots of pockets, including zippered inside security pockets for travel. You will need to have room for a map, compass, sketchbook or journal, writing and drawing implements, a small watercolor box if you choose, travel brushes, sunglasses, camera, mobile phone, or both.

- HEADGEAR: Ball caps offer less UV protection than a crushable, water-resistant, wide-brimmed, round hat. A second option might be angler hats, some of which have larger bills and neck covering to maximize UV protection. A lightweight neck scarf or bandana can be useful for added UV protection.

- FOOTWEAR: Hiking boots are best for treks and trails. Urban explorers may want to acquire a good pair of walking shoes. I personally prefer sturdy, oiled leather ankle-high lace-up boots because they offer maximum lateral support and comfort. Everyone's feet are different. Finding the right fit will require some trial and error. Choose shoes that are appropriate to weather and terrain, with the correct sole tread, insulation, and waterproofing. Because you may be on your feet for hours at a time, comfort is a priority. I also recommend woolen and wool-blend socks for all seasons, because they wick and emit less unpleasant odors after multiple days of wear.

- CLOTHING ACCESSORIES: In certain settings, and at different times of the year, you may want to invest in headgear with insect netting, snake-proof leggings, and a head lamp. I carry a pair of deerskin gloves in all four seasons, only wearing them when necessary. Wearing gloves in winter deprives one's touch of the sensitivity required to write or to paint outdoors. Warm your hand instead inside a rag-wool sock. Then push the butt end of the brush handle or pencil through a gap in the knitting. This allows you to work the tool with bare fingers.

- INSECT REPELLENT & SUNSCREEN: Research your destination. Learn what kinds of biting insects you wish to avoid. Mosquitoes and ticks can transmit unpleasant diseases to humans and animals. Use the appropriate repellent. If you are heading into the north woods, or swimming in tropical waters, you can purchase bear and shark repellent. Likewise, use a maximum strength sunscreen, appropriate to the intensity of the sunlight at your location.

- WATER BOTTLE OR CANTEEN: No piece of equipment is more important. Keeping hydrated is your top priority. I personally do not care for loose cylindrical water bottles, preferring instead to carry water in a more ergonomic nineteenth-century-style military canteen or contemporary hydration pack.

- ACCESSORIES BAG: While a travel vest may replace your shoulder bag, you may opt for extra storage to carry your materials, maps, books, compass, camera, penknife, etc.

WRITING & DRAWING MATERIALS: SKETCHBOOKS

MOLESKINE. Large selection. Strong bindings. Watercolor (landscape format) sketchbooks use archival paper of medium weight and quality. The pocket-sized journal (3.5 x 10 inches) is comparable in size to a mobile phone. Open page-spreads will fit on an A4/8.5x11 flatbed scanner. Gusseted inside-cover back pocket

HAND-BOOK (Kansas City, MO) Global Art Hand-Book Journal. (Landscape format) Fine papers, but bindings can begin to fail before the book is full of entries. Comparable in size to the pocket Moleskine watercolor sketchbook, but thicker. Gusseted inside-cover back pocket

PENTALIC. Aqua Watercolor Sketchbook Journal. Closer in size to the slimmer profile of the Moleskine journal. Produced by a well-known manufacturer of writing and calligraphy supplies.

STRATHMORE. Papers, drawing, and watercolor journals.

WRITING AND DRAWING MATERIALS: TOOLS

KAWECO (Austria)

Sport fountain or ballpoint pen. Hexagonal steel or brass body.

Sketch Up 56 technical pencil. Hexagonal steel or brass body.

Models also come in less durable plastic bodies at lower prices.

SAKURA MICRON (Japan)
Archival waterproof ink. Wonderful for use with ink wash and watercolors. A disposable version of a rapidiograph pen. Sold in black and a wide array of colors and point widths.
PILOT (Japan). Full selection of fine and technical writing instruments.
ROTRING (Germany). Full selection of fine and technical writing instruments.

BRUSHES
DAVINCI Travel brushes.
ESCODA Travel brushes.
RICHESON Plein air watercolor brush set.

WATERCOLORS
L. CORNELISSEN & SON (London). Full selection of pans, tubes, and related materials. Retail walk-in and online sales. https://www.cornelissen.com
GOLDEN PAINTS. The gold standard in acrylic colors for artists, Golden has developed a new line of watercolors marketed as QoR. https://www.qorcolors.com/
KREMER PIGMENTE (Germany & NYC). Selection of travel sets and related materials. Online and walk-in retail sales. https://shop.kremerpigments.com/en/
MAIMERI. Watercolors. Italy. http://www.maimeri.it
SAVOIR-FAIRE. Official representative of Sennelier products in the USA. Also carries a full selection of burshes, papers, and miscellaneous equipment.
SCHMINCKE (Germany). Full selection of watercolors and related materials. Website has a locator for retail outlets. https://www.schmincke.de/en.html
WINDSOR NEWTON (UK & USA). Full selection of watercolors and

related materials widely available. Contact your local art supply store. https://www.winsornewton.com/na/shop

BAGS AND SATCHELS

ORVIS (Manchester, VT): Safe Passage sling pack
C.C. FILSON (Seattle, WA): Small and Medium Field Bags
FROST RIVER (Duluth, MN): Field Satchel
L. CORNELISSEN & SON (London): Leather Artists Sketch Bag

MISCELLANEOUS

WOOD & FAULK: Tripod folding stool

GENERAL OUTDOOR CLOTHING, HIKING, AND CAMPING

L.L. BEAN (ME): General line of outdoor clothing
DULUTH TRADING COMPANY (MN): Travel vests and cargo pants
C.C. FILSON (Seattle, WA): General line of outdoor clothing
ORVIS (Manchester, VT): General line of outdoor clothing
PATAGONIA (California): General line of outdoor clothing
REI: General line of outdoor clothing
TILLEY (Canada): Travel vest and hats

SPECIALTY FOOTWEAR

WOLVERINE: Thousand-Mile Boots
RED WING: Heritage Collection and Hiking Boots
DANNER: Hiking boots
FRYE BOOT COMPANY: Various styles
S.A.S (San Antonio Shoe Co.): Daily footwear

Chapter 7

HUDSON VALLEY RESOURCES: ORGANIZATIONS

APPALACHIAN TRAIL: NEW YORK.
https://appalachiantrail.org/home/explore-the-trail/explore-by-state/new-york

EMPIRE STATE TRAIL.
https://www.ny.gov/programs/empire-state-trail

HIKE THE HUDSON VALLEY.
https://hikethehudsonvalley.com/the-hikes/

HISTORIC HUDSON VALLEY.
https://hudsonvalley.org

HUDSON VALLEY GREENWAY.
https://hudsongreenway.ny.gov

HUDSON VALLEY NATIONAL HERITAGE AREA.
https://www.hudsonrivervalley.com

HUDSON RIVER VALLEY INSTITUTE.
http://www.hudsonrivervalley.org

SCENIC HUDSON.
https://www.scenichudson.org

SLOOP CLEARWATER.
https://www.clearwater.org

RIVERKEEPER.
https://www.riverkeeper.org

JOHN BURROUGHS ASSOCIATION.
https://research.amnh.org/burroughs/slabsides_sanct.html

Chapter 8

HUDSON VALLEY RESOURCES: PARKS AND OPEN SPACES

ADIRONDACK FOREST PRESERVE.
https://www.dec.ny.gov/lands/5263.html

APPALACHIAN TRAIL.
http://www.appalachiantrail.org/home/explore-the-trail/explore-by-state/new-york

BEAR MOUNTAIN STATE PARK.
https://parks.ny.gov/parks/13/details.aspx

CATSKILL FOREST PRESERVE.
https://www.dec.ny.gov/lands/5265.html

CLERMONT. Germantown.
https://parks.ny.gov/historicsites/16/details.aspxhttp:/clermont-statehistoricsite.blogspot.comwww.friendsofclermont.org.

THOMAS COLE NATIONAL HISTORIC SITE. Catskill.
https://thomascole.org

EMPIRE STATE TRAIL.
https://www.ny.gov/programs/empire-state-trail

GATEWAY NATIONAL RECREATION AREA. New York and New Jersey. https://nps.gov/gate/index.htm

HUDSON HIGHLANDS NATURE MUSEUM. Cornwall.
https://www.hhnm.org

HUDSON RIVER MUSEUM. Yonkers.
www.hrm.org

THE LONG PATH.
https://www.nynjtc.org/region/long-path

MIINNEWASKA STATE PARK. Kerhonkson.
https://parks/ny.gov/parks/minnewaska/details.aspx

MOHONK MOUNTAIN HOUSE. New Paltz.
www.mohonkpreserve.org

MOHONK PRESERVE. New Paltz.
https://parks.ny.gov/regions/palisades/default.aspx
NEW YORK CITY DEPARTMENT OF PARKS AND RECREATION.
https://nycgovparks.org
NORTH-SOUTH LAKE. Haines Falls.
https://hikethehudsonvalley.com/hikes/
north-south-lake-north-point/
FREDERIC CHURCH'S OLANA. Greenport.
https://www.olana.org
PALISADES INTERSTATE PARK: NEW JERSEY.
http://www.njpalisades.org
PALISADES INTERSTATE PARK: NEW YORK.
https://parks.ny.gov/regions/palisades/default.aspx
PHILLIPSE MANOR. Sleepy Hollow.
http://www.philipsemanor.org
POET'S WALK. Annandale.
https://www.scenichudson.org/parks/poetswalk
HOME OF FRANKLIN D. ROOSEVELT. Hyde Park.
https://www.nps.gov/hofr/index.htm
SAM'S LEAP. Cragsmoor.
https://hikethehudsonvalley.com/hikes/sams-point/
SARATOGA NATIONAL HISTORICAL PARK.
https://www.nps.gov/sara.index.htm
SLABSIDES. West Park.
http://www.johnburroughsassociation.org
TALLMAN STATE PARK.
https://parks.ny.gov/parks/119/details.aspx
VANDERBILT MANSION NATIONAL HISTORIC SITE. Hyde Park.
https://www.nps.gov/vama/index.htm
WALKWAY ACROSS THE HUDSON. Poughkeepsie.
https://walkway.org

Chapter 9
READING LIST

A note to the reader: Below is a list of special-interest books one is unlikely to find at every bookstore or visitor center. Some are available online. Others may have to be requested through interlibrary loan. Some have been made available as free downloads online, or as print-on-demand facsimile editions. You are encouraged to follow your own interest, whether that be hiking, angling, or camping, or science, history, or art. All these narratives are intertwined. Follow the path that rises to your feet. When stopping to rest, have something great to read.

HUDSON VALLEY

Catlin, Daniel, Jr. *The Hudson River Portfolio.* William Guy Wall and John Agg. Published by the author. Book design and printing by Southbury Printing Centre, Southbury, CT. (A facsimile of the 1821–25 series of prints and texts, based on a Hudson River journey completed in 1820)

Dunwell, Frances F. *The Hudson: America's River.* New York: Columbia University Press. 2008

Dunwell, Frances F. *The Hudson River Highlands.* New York: Columbia University Press. 1991

Foster, Kathleen. *Captain Watson's Travels in America.* Barra Foundation. University of Pennsylvania Press, Philadelphia. 1997. (A British naval officer's sketchbooks produced during travels along the Schuylkill and Hudson Rivers in 1816-17)

Hamerton, Philip Gilbert. *A Painter's Camp, in Three Books.* Roberts Brothers. Boston. 1867. (British artist describes working en plein air during the mid-19th century)

Herbert, Kari, and Huw Lewis-Jones. *Explorers' Sketchbooks. The Art of Discovery and Adventure.* Foreword by Robert Macfarlane. Thames & Hudson. London and New York. 2016. (An overview of expeditionary sketchbook art from ca. 1580-1920)

Lossing, Benson J. *The Hudson: From the Wilderness to the Sea.* Introduction by Pete Seeger. Black Dome Press. Hensonville, New York. Originally published in 1866 by H.B. Nims & Co., Troy New York. (Firsthand account by a travel writer and his wife of a Hudson River journey in 1859)

Manthorne, Katherine E. *Tropical Renaissance. North American Artists Exploring Latin America 1839-1879.* Smithsonian. 1989. (Artists of the Hudson River School painting Latin America)

Manthorne, Katherine E. (editor) *Landscapes of Latin America from the Collection of Patricia Phelps de Cisneros. CPPC.* New York. 2015 (Traveler-artists drawn to South America by the spirit of adventure)

Marley, Dr. Anna O. *Schuylkill to the Hudson: Landscapes of the Early Republic.* Pennsylvania Academy of the Fine Arts. Philadelphia. 2019

Owens, Gwendolyn. *Visions of Nature: Artists and the Environment.* Picturing America. Lithographs by Jacques-Gerard Milbert. Lake Tear of the Clouds to New York City. A Hudson River Journey by Don Nice. Exhibition catalogue. Albany Institute of History and Art. Albany, New York. 1991. (This exhibition celebrated a French artist who traveled the Hudson in the 1830s, and a (then) living American artist who traveled by inflatable boat from the mountains to New York harbor)

Peale, Rembrandt. *Graphics: A Manual of Drawing and Writing for the Use of Schools and Families.* J.P. Peaslee. New York. 1835. (The first widely read how-to book on drawing and penmanship, taught to all at one time. Available as downloads and print-on-demand)

Peck, Daniel. *Thomas Cole's Refrain. Paintings of Catskill Creek.* Cornell University Press. Ithaca, New York. 2018

Schuyler, David. *Sanctified Landscape: Writers, Artists and the Hudson River Valley.* Cornell University Press. Ithaca, New York. 2012. (An excellent cultural history of the Hudson Valley)

Schuyler, David. *Embattled River: The Hudson and Modern American Environmentalism.* Cornell University Press. Ithaca, New York. 2018. (History of pollution and remediation of the Hudson)

Walker, Charlotte. *The Art of Seeing Things. Essays by John Burroughs.* Syracuse University Press, Syracuse, New York. 2001. (Insightful writings by one of 19th-century America's leading environmentalists)

Whisenhurst, William Benton. *A Russian Paints America: The Travels of Pavel P. Svin'in. 1811-1813.* McGill-Queens University Press. Montreal. 2008. (Travels and artworks by the first Russian ambassador to the U.S.)

GENERAL INTEREST

Brown, David Blayney. *J.M.W. Turner. The 'Skies" Sketchbook.* (Facsimile). Tate Publishing. London. 2017

Butlin, Martin. *Samuel Palmer Sketchbook of 1824*. Thames and Hudson. London. 2004

Catlin, Daniel Jr. *Hudson River Port-Folio*. Facsimile Edition. Catlin. Southbury, CT. 2010

Cooperman, Emily T. *County Seats of the United States. William Russell Birch*. University of Pennsylvania Press. Philadelphia. 2009

Cremieux, Therese & Holzwarth, Hans Werner. *Bon Voyage: Francoise Gilot's Travel Sketchbooks*. (facsimile) Three volumes. Taschen. 2016

Davis, Earl. *Stuart Davis Sketchbooks*. (facsimile) Estate of Stuart Davis, Grace Borgenicht Gallery and The Arts Publisher. New York. 18=986

Foster, Kathleen. *Captain Watson's Travels in America. The Sketchbooks and Diaries pf Joshua Rowley Watson*. The Barra Foundation and University of Pennsylvania Press. 1997.

Herbert, Karl & Lewis-Jones, Hu. *Explorers' Sketchbooks: The Art of Discovery & Adventure*. Chronicle Press. Thames & Hudson. London. 2016, 2017

Hockney, David. *A Yorkshire Sketchbook*. (facsimile) Royal Academy of Art. London. 2012

Houston, Kenneth. *The Book*. W.W. Norton. New York & London. 2016

Johnson, Eugene J. *Drawn from the Source. The Travel Sketches of Louis Kahn*. Williams College Museum of Art. Williamstown. Massachusetts. 1996

Levine, David & Sloan, Mrs. John. Edited by Mill Roseman. *A Sketchbook of Maurice Prendergast.* (facsimile) Hammermill Papers Group. Erie, Pennsylvania. 1974

Mendelsohn, Janet & Wilson, Chris. *Drawn to Landscape: The Pioneering Work of J.B. Jackson.* George F. Thompson Publishing. University of Virginia Press. 2015

Michener, James A. *The Hokusai Sketchbooks* (a classic). Charles Tuttle. Rutland VT. Multiple editions

Morgan, Robert C. *Will Barnet. A Sketchbook, 1932-1934.* (facsimile0 George Braziller. 2009

Sciré, Giovanna Negri. *Canaletto's Sketchbooks.* (facsimile). Canal & Stamperia Editrice. Venice. 1997

Smee, Sebastian. *Lucian Freud Drawings 1940.* Matthew Marks Gallery. New York. 2003

Stewart, Harris B. & Henderson, J. Welles. *Challenger Sketchbook.* Philadelphia Maritime Museum. 1972

Vellekoop, Marje & Suijver, Renske. *Vincent van Gogh. The Sketchbooks.* Limited Edition Facsimile in Solander Cloth Case. Folio Society & the Van Gogh Museum.

Wick, Peter A. *A Summer Sketchbook. David Levine.* (facsimile) Mitchell Press. New York. 1963.

This book is for my beloved wife and brilliant partner,

Kathie Manthorne

This book was inspired by historic and contemporary expeditionary artists too numerous to mention here. Readers will find them in these pages. For their various contributions to my efforts in assembling this book, and the projects upon which it is based, I am deeply grateful to the Pollock Krasner Foundation for the 2017 grant, which provided much-needed support to complete pending projects. I am also indebted to a number of remarkable individuals, including my personal editor, Pamela Barr; content editor Peggy Kellar at Schiffer Publishing; the late Charles C. Bergman; Independence Seaport Museum chief curator Craig Bruns; Boscobel House and Gardens executive director Jennifer Carlquist; Andrew Drabkin; Joseph Goddu; American Philosophical Society curator emeritus Roy Goodman; Albany Institute of History and Art executive director Tammis K. Groft; Maria Hajic, Evan Feldman, and John Macker of Gerald Peters Gallery and Peters Projects Santa Fe; Colonel James Johnson, US Army, retired, of the Hudson Valley Institute at Marist University; Eakins Press Foundation executive director Peter Kayafas; noted author and plein-air wizard James Howard Kunstler; Joe Langman and publisher Pete Schiffer of Schiffer Publishing; Cathy and David Lilburne of Antipodean Books; Institute Library New Haven resident curator Martha Willette Lewis; Hudson River Museum deputy director Saralinda Lichtblau; Robert and Roberta Lyons; Steven Miller; Barnabas McHenry; Fort Montgomery State History Site director Grant Miller; Teresa O'Dea; Irina Orlova; William E. Podszus, Esq.; USMA West Point Museum executive director David Reel; Janet Wilson Smith; Don Stinson; Fine Art Connoisseur executive editor Peter Trippi; Hudson River Museum executive director Masha Turchinsky; chair of the Curatorial Department, Laura Vookles, at Hudson River Museum; Graham White of Digital Media Design; and David G. Wright of the Association of Print Scholars, with special thanks to my late mother and our supportive family. Thank you all!